The Fiction of André Pieyre de Mandiargues

André Pieyre de Mandiargues by Bona, 1950, used by permission

The Fiction of André Pieyre de Mandiargues

David J. Bond

SYRACUSE UNIVERSITY PRESS   1982

Library of Congress Cataloging in Publication Data

Bond, David J.
   The fiction of André Pieyre de Mandiargues.

   Bibliography: p.
   Includes index.
   1. Pieyre de Mandiargues, André, 1909–   —Criti-
cism and interpretation.   I. Pieyre de Mandiargues,
André, 1909–   . II. Title.
PQ2631.I49Z56   1982   843'.914   82-5894
   ISBN 978-0-8156-2283-3   AACR2

Contents

DAVID J. BOND received the Ph.D. from the University of London and is Associate Professor of French, University of Saskatchewan. His articles have appeared in *The International Fiction Review, Studies in Twentieth-Century Literature*, and *Canadian Literature*.

/

Foreword

QUITE APART FROM ANY QUESTION OF PRIDE or modesty, there is still a writer in me, and that writer would have great difficulty concealing the pleasure he derived from reading the book that David J. Bond has written about him: *The Fiction of André Pieyre de Mandiargues*. For I believe that a very substantial difference is to be made between articles of literary criticism, even when highly favorable to one's work, or strictly academic studies whose main purpose is to meet the scrutiny of colleagues, and a book in which a line of thought is pursued, understanding and style emerge, and in which a kind of love is revealed. This word will perhaps be considered in bad taste by some readers, but I have engaged in critical activity enough myself to know that one really understands only what one loves, and that understanding, that is to say a true grasp, of the work of a poet, a novelist, a painter, or a sculptor has no source beyond a passionate interest, which is a type of love. For a creative artist, of whatever kind, nothing is so moving as to realize that he and his work have become "objects of love." I do not think I am mistaken when I say that I experienced that flattering emotion as I observed, chapter by chapter, page by page, word by word, my reflection, and the reflection of my writing, taking shape in the ample mirror of David J. Bond's sensitive and meticulous book, which often sent me back in time, bringing me again to the wonderful moments of inspiration and composition. Any careful reader of my stories will, I think, have gathered that for me the world of the imagination and the world of outside reality form an immense double mirror in which reflections interplay and are prolonged to infinity, giving me a sense of inspiration that I would like to pass on to my readers. Let me, then, express here my gratitude to David J. Bond for having entered so fully into my arrangement of mirrors and for having produced this fine, clear, original book about my somewhat fantastical creations. Meanwhile, I await that anonymous dust that I know very well my work will become, and I with it.

Spring 1982   ANDRÉ PIEYRE DE MANDIARGUES

Avant-Propos

TOUT ORGUEIL OU TOUTE modestie mis à part, l'écrivain que je suis encore aurait bien du mal à dissimuler le bonheur qu'il a retiré de la lecture du livre à lui consacré par David J. Bond: *The Fiction of André Pieyre de Mandiargues*. Car il me semble qu'une différence très grande existe entre des articles de critique littéraire, fussent-ils hautement favorables à votre œuvre, ou des études strictement universitaires qui ont pour but principal de satisfaire à des examens professoraux, et un livre où s'exprime une pensée, où s'affirment une intelligence et un style, où se déclare une sorte d'amour. Ce dernier mot, certains le trouveront de mauvais goût peut-être, mais j'ai assez pratiqué, moi aussi, la critique, pour savoir que l'on ne comprend vraiment que ce que l'on aime et que l'intelligence, c'est-à-dire l'entendement, de l'œuvre d'un poète, d'un romancier, d'un peintre ou d'un sculpteur, n'a d'autre source qu'un intérêt passionné, qui est une catégorie de l'amour. Pour un créateur, quel qu'il soit, rien n'est aussi émouvant que de constater que son œuvre et lui-même sont devenus des "objets aimés." Je ne crois pas me tromper en disant que j'ai eu cette flatteuse émotion tandis que je suivais, chapitre après chapitre, page après page, mot après mot, le développement de mon image et de celle de mes écrits dans le grand miroir du livre sensible et minutieux de David J. Bond, qui souvent me faisait remonter le temps en me ramenant aux belles époques de l'inspiration et de la rédaction. Tout bon lecteur de mes récits, je crois, aura saisi que pour moi le monde imaginaire et celui de la réalité extérieure forment un double et immense miroir où le jeu des reflets se prolonge infiniment, en me donnant une illumination que je voudrais donner à mes lecteurs. Qu'il me soit donc permis de dire ici à David J. Bond ma reconnaissance pour être entré si profondément dans mon jeu de miroirs et pour avoir produit sur le sujet de mes inventions plus ou moins fantastiques ce beau livre original et clair. En attendant cette poussière anonyme que je sais bien que vont devenir mon œuvre et moi-même.

Printemps 1982   ANDRÉ PIEYRE DE MANDIARGUES

Introduction

TO READ THE FICTION of André Pieyre de Mandiargues is to enter a very special realm—a world of fantasy where the rules of everyday logic no longer apply and where anything may happen. Characters shrink in size; a man is transported to the sea bed, where he comes face to face with a giant goddess; mysterious women suddenly appear and lure the male characters to their destruction; a girl sees her future acted out by phantom players in the window of a nearby building; three minute female figures emerge from a stone and perform a ritual dance.[1] The reader is never quite sure what surprises a tale by Mandiargues might hold, and his sense of curiosity is continually aroused.

The dreamlike atmosphere of much of this fiction also contributes to its attraction, for Mandiargues excels in the evocation of oneiric visions. There is, for example, the wedding ceremony descibed in "Le Casino patibulaire," one of the stories in *Le Musée noir*. We see the dreamer walking to the altar between rows of black-clad pilgrims holding candles aloft, and "the candelabras lean inwards, the candles meet above the heads of the procession, joining together in hissing streams of soft substance that soon sets in long, pale, translucent stalactites; the whole mass rises from earth to heaven in an immense cathedral of dripping wax and smoky flames, while the chords of a titanic organ mingle with the ringing of bells and the murmuring of the pilgrims." Then there are the experiences of the hero of *Marbre*, who dreams that he is watching a giant plunging a child into a tub of cuttlefish while chanting fragments of the Song of Songs; that he is paralyzed by some unseen power as a girl paints his portrait on a mirror, and he is then obliged to adopt every gesture and assume every pose that she wills on him; that he is carried to an island on a silent, black-draped craft propelled by three women whose song is accompanied by the howling of the wind.

Amidst the dreams and visions, monsters and demons often appear. In *Soleil des loups* there are two stories in which such creatures are depicted. The hero of "L'Archéologue" encounters an enormous female who both repels and attracts him, and who cannot be human "for her gigantic proportions, her dark coloring, and the veneer of her glistening skin make her seem like a bronze statue." Captain Idalium in "L'Opéra des falaises" meets a group of demon-like beings, "urchins who were closer to dogs, monkeys or bear cubs than to the offspring of man." In a story from *Le Musée noir* called "Le passage Pommeraye," an "alligator-man" is discovered wrapped in a piece of crimson carpet, badly wounded, lying among the ordures in a gutter, and uttering cries like those of an abandoned baby.

Mandiargues has an imagination of great inventive power. Dream, unexpected events, monsters, and unusual creatures of all kinds combine to produce the sort of atmosphere found in few modern writers. But it is above all the language in which this fantasy is expressed that creates the special flavor of his works. His style ranges from the sensuous description in *Le Lis de mer* of lilies which give off "an extraordinarily potent perfume, simultaneously fragrant and heavy, acidic and sickly-sweet, all-pervading, something between the high-pitched note produced by the spring narcissus and the lower one of the autumn amaryllis" to the precise geometric description of a tiny man in "Le Diamant," one of the stories in *Feu de braise*, a man who stands "holding his arms and legs spread apart so that the extremities of his hands and feet formed the four corners of a square . . . while his navel, at the point of intersection of the diagonals that one might have drawn, coincided exactly with the center of this imaginary square."

Often Mandiargues's descriptions are of wildly baroque scenes, such as the interior of the palace described in "Le Tombeau d'Aubrey Beardsley," a story from *Le Musée noir*. Here we are shown a kind of "cavern, as radiant as a soap bubble floating above the earth on a lattice of transparent chains." Its walls are covered with mirrors, and "a forest of twisting staircases linked together a two-story construction paved with blocks of light gray lava alternating with ones of dark blue marble and which was also walled with mirrors . . . having so many square or circular openings in them that they formed a thicket of bridges, knots, crosses and stars." Other passages convey the charm of strange objects, such as the marble clock described in *Le Cadran lunaire*, a mixture of car radiator and miniature tomb containing an intricate mechanism of cogwheels that are "square (almost), elliptical, lopsided, oval, star-shaped (with four points and composed of two superimposed ellipses)."

No translation can capture the poetic charm of Mandiargues's writing, and no enumeration of its characteristics can convey its appeal to the imagination. It is, however, an appeal that literary juries have more than once recognized, for *Soleil des loups* was awarded the *Prix des critiques* in 1951, *Feu de braise* won the *Prix de la nouvelle* in 1959, and *La Marge* earned the most prestigious of all French literary prizes in 1967: the *Prix Goncourt*. In 1981, his work as a whole was honored by the *Aigle d'or des écrivains* at the Festival de Nice.

Mandiargues has always been held in high esteem by professional critics, and there is hardly a review of his works which does not praise some aspects of them. His style especially has been singled out for favorable comment. He has been called "one of the rare stylists of our contemporary literature," and is said to have the "most crystal-clear style of all contemporary French writers." One critic talks of his "precise, rigorous style . . . which is also, however, at the same time, sumptuous, torrential and inspired," and another says that he writes in "the great tradition of classical prose in which proportion and mastery are combined." Others have remarked on the sensuous power of his writing: "There is, in the works of this distinguished writer, the deeply sensuous magic of . . . . a sweet but slightly over-ripe fruit," and "One notes throughout his works prose cadences worthy of Bossuet or Bourdaloue, rhythmic forms into which are poured, like gold and silver, the verbal counterparts of his sensations."[2]

The compelling, magical nature of Mandiargues's world has also been noted by critics, who have called him "diviner of the unusual" and have referred to his works as "a kingdom where the unusual reigns supreme." They say that "everyone acknowledges the beauty of the poet's (in the broadest sense of the word) imagination" and that his goal is "to reveal the world in a new light." The haunting dream world that he produces is "a strange yet familiar universe" and leads another critic to call him "The great poet of oneiric prose." He is a "superbly evocative writer" who creates a sphere in which "a certain quality in the atmosphere brings about a different refraction and a new rhythm in the movements of the body and the soul." In Mandiargues's writing "sites and characters are imprinted on the imagination by their unusual nature. It is not possible, once one has encountered them, to forget their disturbing appearance or their uncertain yet obvious reality."[3]

Several critics consider Pieyre de Mandiargues one of the most original writers of today. Edmond Jaloux has called him "the most totally original of his generation,"[4] and Octavio Paz says he is "one of the truly original writers to have appeared in France since World War Two." Jean d'Ormesson writes: "André Pieyre de Mandiargues may be placed, without any doubt, in the very front rank of our writers today." To conclude this panegyric from the critics, one might quote Robert Kanters, who says of Mandiargues: "He is . . . among the very small number of writers who are an honor to literature at the present time."[5]

These are just a few comments taken from reviews and criticisms of Mandiargues's works, but they show the kind of praise that his books attract. Yet, outside the circle of professional critics, Mandiargues is not at all well-known; outside of France, he is almost unknown. What is equally puzzling is that, despite the approval of his work displayed by so many critics, no overall study of his fiction has yet been undertaken.[6]

Speculation as to why this should be so would be futile. It is unlikely to produce a convincing answer, and would do nothing to make his works better known. A more sensible course of action would be to set about producing an introductory study of his fiction, a study that might be a first modest step toward bringing him to the notice of a slightly wider public. That is what this book attempts to do.

The difficulty lies in the complexity of Mandiargues's works and in the breadth of his vision. They are susceptible of many interpretations and approaches, all of them equally valid. The few themes that I have picked out here are but some of the more striking aspects of his work. They are not picked out at random, however. Once one becomes acquainted with Mandiargues's fiction it is apparent that there are certain recurring patterns in his fantasy. From one story to another, erotic incidents occur that are also related to a particular feeling toward the natural world; a fascination with geometrical shapes and symmetry is also evident; certain rituals and ceremonies are to be found in many works; time is often manipulated in a particular way; characters in different works undergo very similar changes of shape or size. Mandiargues is far too conscious a manipulator of his medium for these patterns to be accidental. I have tried, therefore, to show not only where these patterns occur, but *why* they do so.[7]

After the work of Freud, Jung, Frye, Eliade, and several others, we know that fantasy often hides a very serious intent. It is frequently used to examine some of the oldest, most persistent preoccupations of mankind. As one writer on the fantastic, Marcel Schneider, puts it: "The fantastic allows the writer to describe in concrete terms, in tangible images, with everyday tales, the problems that concern us all: time, destiny, the beyond, the face of God, salvation, love."[8] By organizing his fantasy into certain patterns, Mandiargues too is telling us something about such fundamental human concerns as the relationship of life to death, man's eternal mystical urge to escape the limits of his self, the mysterious forces both within us and in the world around us, and the essential polarity of human experience.

The suspicion that Mandiargues's tales of fantasy exist on more than a merely literal level is supported by the fact that he was, for some years, associated with the surrealists, and, although he no longer counts himself one of them, he has never ceased to express his admiration for them.[9] The surrealists, among their many new perspectives on the world, made a distinction between the manifest and the latent content of things, saying that the writer should attempt to reveal the latter. They argued that the imagination should be freed and that we should abandon rigidly rational attitudes toward the world in order to see things in a new light. Is not Mandiargues, in his strangely dreamlike and irrational tales, inviting us to do just that? His use of fantasy may be seen as an attempt to make us look beyond the utilitarian assumptions of everyday life and see the latent content, the hidden face of the reality that he describes.

An incident in Mandiargues's novel *La Marge* sums up perfectly what he would like us to do. Sigismond, the hero of the novel, is lying in his hotel room when he hears someone in the street crying out a word that sounds like *parabole*. He suspects, however, that his ears are misleading him, and, not satisfied with the evidence of his senses, he goes into the street to find out what the word actually is. This whole episode is itself a parable, one which teaches us to look beyond what is immediately apparent. The edifice that our senses construct for us, Mandiargues writes in his preface to *Le Musée noir*, is not always a very solid wall. Those who are willing to abandon utilitarian attitudes will pierce the wall and gain access to another reality. This is especially true when there is "a climate favorable to the transfiguration of phenomena felt by the senses." It is this climate that Mandiargues creates in his fiction.

The invitation to look beyond the literal meaning of his stories is counterbalanced by an implied warning. Like the surrealists, Mandiargues is not very fond of critics who try to find systems and categories in works of art. He sees little difference between them and despots who force political or social systems on people, and in *Troisième Belvédère* he mounts several attacks on "classifications laboriously built by school-teachers and barracks-masters." He is particularly scathing about academic critics who court a reputation as radicals by rejecting all art that does not fit a preconceived system. He seems to think that American critics are especially prone to doing this, and in *Le Désordre de la mémoire* he calls them "professors whose stomachs are ulcerated by the sinister Coca-Cola." One reason why he praises the surrealists is that there were no professors among them. Unfortunately, he continues, surrealism itself is now an object of research and is "in the hands of academic pedants and modish profiteers." In *Le Cadran lunaire*, Mandiargues, despite (or because of) his several volumes of literary and art criticism, is at pains to dissociate himself from such "critics, weighers of syllables, doctors of hot air, hair-splitting executioners, voyeurs of inspiration."

Speaking as an academic who has spent some time looking for patterns in Mandiargues's work, I find these remarks rather daunting, but I console myself with the thoughts that I like Mandiargues's work very much, that my purpose here is not to attack it, that it is because I am fascinated by his fiction that I want to see what lies behind it, and that I am not trying to make it fit any preconceived categories. (Besides which, I am not American and I do not like Coca-Cola.) In any case, although Mandiargues attacks a certain type of literary critic, he is a critic himself, and he even encourages those who would try to interpret works of art. He argues in *Troisième Belvédère* that, once it has been produced, a work of art exists independently of its creator and that "critical work has the right and the duty to judge and interpret in an original way what it examines." He has even said, according to Alain Jouffroy: "I am very glad, of course, to have the most diverse interpretations placed on my books, provided they are intelligent ones."[10]

In his own critical articles, Mandiargues refuses to speak ill of works and rejects the "compulsory slander" that he finds in much modern criticism.[11] He says in *Le Cadran lunaire*: "Whether it be books, theatre or painting, dance or cuisine, music if I am not too inexpert, I like to speak only of what is of high quality, of what is good, of what has moved me." My own reasons for writing about Pieyre de Mandiargues are the same. His books have moved and fascinated me, and it is only because they have done this that I wish to write about them.

I have not set myself an easy task. As I have already indicated, Mandiargues's work is complex and has a multitude of ramifications. Since this is a general introduction to his fiction and since he is not well-known, I have begun with a biographical sketch before moving on, in the second chapter, to one of the most striking and immediatly obvious elements of his fiction: its erotic content. I have linked this eroticism to the use of ritual and to the characters' curious relationship to the world around them. In the third chapter, I have examined the role of sex in his novels in relation to death and the passing of time. Chapter 4 deals with the desire displayed by many of his characters to escape from the self, and I have then shown how this desire is connected to a dualistic, almost Manichaean view of life. Chapters 5 and 6 discuss the use of mythical motifs in Mandiargues's fiction. I have pointed out that much of his work recounts a mythical quest ending in union with a deity who represents the forces of creation. The characterization in his fiction, his handling of time, of geometric designs, and his dualistic conception of life are all linked to his use of mythical patterns. In chapter 7, I examine Mandiargues's work as a symbolic journey into the self. Chapter 8 deals with his use of detail, his description of objects, and how he ties his fantasy to the real world. It then goes on to his view of the artist as a *voyant* or a medium for forces released in his work, and I have discussed how these ideas are associated with certain surrealist views. In my conclusion, I have tried to show Mandiargues's relationship to other contemporary French writers, and especially to the surrealists.

I have not attempted to analyze or even to mention all of Mandiargues's fiction, since there is far too much to be included in a study of this nature. I have based my comments on his novels and on the longer pieces of fiction. Certain shorter stories have also been mentioned because they illustrate particularly well the point that I wish to make. The many stories that I have not mentioned, or to which I have only briefly referred, do, however, provide supporting evidence for the points that I have made. The themes and patterns that I have examined are to be found throughout Mandiargues's writings.

      One final word: Since Mandiargues's fiction is not well-known (with the possible exception of *La Marge*, because it won the *Prix Goncourt*, and of *La Motocyclette*, where the erotic content and the fact that it has been made into a film have brought it to the attention of a wider public), I have been obliged in the following pages to give summaries of his stories and novels when first mentioning them. I have kept these summaries as brief as is consistent with an understanding of the important characteristics of the works in question, and I hope that this will aid rather than interrupt the flow of the arguments. All translations of quotations, whether from Mandiargues's work or others, are my own, unless otherwise indicated.

1

A Biographical Sketch

Beauté, que pour maîtresse unique j'ai choisie. Ronsard

ANDRÉ PIEYRE DE MANDIARGUES'S LIFE is one of exemplary dedication to his art. He has, through the years, shown an unbending will to create the most perfect art of which he is capable, and he has placed this before all concern for popularity or commercial success. The consideration uppermost in his mind has always been to develop his own skills and to produce flawless work. So concerned was he with his own exacting standards that he never even considered publishing his writing before the age of thirty-four. Until that time, he underwent a self-imposed apprenticeship during which he was constantly writing and attempting to perfect his style.[1]

Mandiargues was born in Paris in 1909 into what appears to have been a fairly affluent family. He had one brother, six years younger than himself. Their father was killed in the First World War, in 1916, leaving them to the care of their mother and a governess. Under these circumstances, his mother was naturally a very important force in the formation of Mandiargues's tastes and attitudes. She was also a woman of strong character, and this made her influence over him even greater. His love of art may be traced, to a large extent, to this influence, for she was well acquainted with the world of art. She was born in 1880, the youngest child of Paul Berard, who was a friend of Renoir and Monet. While still a child, she had become used to seeing artists such as these in her home, and she served as a model for several of Renoir's portraits, including *L'Enfant blanc*. Mandiargues has carried on what is almost a family tradition through his friendship with many artists and his writings on art.

Although his mother undoubtedly influenced him in his initial taste for art, she did not approve of the particular kind of art that he came to like the most. He says with some sadness that she never really understood the avant-garde and the revolutionary art that he has always especially appreciated. While it would be dangerous to see this rejection of what he loved as the only reason for the way he depicts women in his

1

fiction, there may be some connection. To have his tastes repudiated by a mother whom he cherished must have influenced the archetypal image of woman that he creates in his work. By showing many of his women characters as docile, passive creatures to be used by men almost as they wish, he may be reacting against this rejection and affirming his own freedom and will to choose.[2]

An equally important influence on his childhood was that of his Swiss governess, who had also looked after his mother when she was a child. Marie Schoeni, whom he always called Mie, is remembered by him with as much affection as his mother. The memory of her has remained so firmly with him that he has used her as a model for Sigismond's governess in *La Marge* and for Jean de Juni's in "L'Enfantillage," one of the stories in *Feu de braise*. She was, he says in *Le Désordre de la mémoire*, "so good, so simple, so modest, so wise, so pure that she stays in my memory as a kind of saint." Mie taught him to love the natural world, especially the sea and the seashore. He says that "it is to old Mie's simple teaching that I owe the knowledge and the great love of nature that are part of me, that quest for universal love which is my best quality and without which my inspiration, even my imagination could not exist." This love of nature lies behind some of Mandiargues's best work.

As a child, he was thin and unhealthy. He was timid and stuttered when under emotional stress. He does not appear to have enjoyed school and spent much of his time surreptitiously reading during classes. His brightest memories are of holidays that his family took on the coast of Normandy. His mother owned an old house there, and he spent the happiest days of his childhood at Puys, Le Pollet, and Berneval exploring the rocks and fishing in the pools left by the retreating tide. The white chalk cliffs exercised a particular fascination for him and have found their way into more than one of his works: they are alluded to in the title of his volume of poetry *L'Age de craie*, and they appear in such short stories as "La Marée," "Mascarets," and "L'Opéra des falaises."

Although he loved books, the awe in which he held the art of writing prevented Mandiargues from believing that he could ever be a writer. He says that when he was a child and an adolescent, "my love of books made me consider writers as beings so superior to the rest of humanity that it would have been ridiculous, idiotic, or criminal to aspire to elevate myself one day to their ranks." The first authors to attract his admiration were Pierre Loti, Jules Verne, and Paul d'Ivoi. (Even today he praises Loti's style and says that he is an under-estimated writer.) At the age of fourteen, he read Gide's *Les Nourritures terrestres*, and, shortly after this, he read Nietzsche and Valery Larbaud during mathematics and physics classes. Gradually, despite his belief that he could never produce work of any value, he began to write too. His first piece of any length, *La*

Chair et le diable, Flesh and the Devil, was a libretto written in 1929 for a young English girl whom he met in Vienna. The first poem that he can remember writing was composed at Berneval for a girl whom he had seen on the beach. The importance of woman as inspiration for his work is already evident in these first two forays into literary creation.

Mandiargues was obviously not the keenest of pupils, and even when he became a university student he spent his time translating William Carlos Williams during lectures. He passed his baccalauréat examination after several attempts, and was persuaded by his mother to prepare the entrance competition for the Ecole des Hautes Etudes Commerciales. After failing at his first attempt, he was accepted by what he calls "that sinister school," and he embarked on commercial studies. In view of his non-conformism, his often expressed anti-bourgeois feelings, and his left-wing sympathies, it is amusing to think of him studying for a business career. Not surprisingly, he did not do very well, and he proclaims himself "not displeased at having been the only student in my year not to be promoted from the first to the second year." He abandoned this establishment and registered for a literature degree at the Sorbonne, but he did not pursue these studies beyond the first examination.

Speaking of this time in his life, Mandiargues says in *Le Désordre de la mémoire:* "When I think of those far-off years, 1927, 1928, 1929, I have to recognize within me a certain avid desire to live, dominated by a morbid tendency to waste my life."

His apparent lack of ambition and "serious" intent made his relationship with his mother difficult. She did not know that he was beginning secretly to write, but, if she had, Mandiargues says that she would have tried to make this into a "serious" career. She would have used her influence to get him a position in a publishing house, to tie him to a regular and respectable routine. This was the last thing he wanted.

When he reached the age of twenty-one, Mandiargues came into a modest inheritance from his father that gave him some financial independence and enabled him to live more or less as he wished. He had already been to Italy when he was about seventeen; now he was able to travel again. From 1931 onwards he visited Germany, Poland, Austria, Hungary, Romania, other parts of the Balkans, and, of course, Italy—a country that he loved from his very first visit and that he claims to know better than his own. On several of these journeys he was accompanied by his first great friend, Henri Cartier-Bresson, who was later to achieve success as a photographer.

Mandiargues had few friends at this time, however. He has always been plagued by what he calls "that enormous, immense timidity, a real neurosis of which I was a victim for many years, and which still persists." He believes that, by writing, he has rid himself of most of this timidity, but, in the years before he published anything, it made his life miserable. He lived, he says, "in a kind of pit from which I could not get out." The outward sign of his nervous anxieties was his stuttering, which almost disappeared in the 1940s but which occasionally affects him even now. Although many practitioners of psychoanalysis attribute this speech problem to childhood trauma, Mandiargues can find no such explanation in his own childhood, except, perhaps, the death of his father. However, although he never mentions his mother's attitude to his artistic tastes, this clearly could be another possible reason.

It was due, no doubt, in large measure to his timidity that he kept his first literary productions secret. His sporadic writing became a regular activity from the time he was twenty-three, but he still told nobody: neither his family nor his closest friend Cartier-Bresson nor even his acquaintances in the literary world knew about it. At first, the idea of publishing his work seems not to have entered his head: "I had no ambition to become a professional writer, nor even a recognized poet; I had no concern to procure any kind of success for myself." He wrote for his own pleasure, and with the intention of perfecting his style. He also viewed the many books that he avidly read as a means of improving his writing, and he looks back on those years as ones of invaluable preparation.

Mandiargues rejects the currently fashionable idea that all writers are inspired by the need to communicate with others. He calls this a "scholastic and inadequate explanation."[3] He believes that his own writings are more of an attempt to communicate with himself. Consequently, he is unable to understand or to sympathize with many young writers whose only desire is to publish, to see themselves in print, and thus to justify their existence. He condemns their lack of patience, their unwillingness to undertake a long, slow learning process, and their anger when their first efforts are not immediately published. He believes that many modern painters fall into the same trap because they seek the easiest course, not realizing that artistic creation involves struggle, anguish, and patience. He says: "Their art is too facile. An artist must work, strain, know anguish in order to create. Today painters think that the easy way is the right way. Art must be difficult. There is a time during the creative process when inspiration should explode—as the surrealists stated. But after this initial burst of intuition, the artist—like the artisan—must labor. Facility leads to sterility. That's one of the reasons I like the new writers like Ricardou. They at least have made things difficult."[4]

It was during the Second World War that Mandiargues finally overcame his reluctance to publish. He spent this time in Monte Carlo, living a solitary life devoted to the contemplation of dreams. He had always been fascinated by dreams, and his interest was further stimulated when, one day, he discovered in an antiquarian book shop in Nice a work by the nineteenth-century writer the Marquis d'Hervey Saint-Denys: *Les Rêves et les moyens de les diriger*. Inspired by this work, he set about systematically provoking dreams by the use of coca leaves provided by a friendly pharmacist. He would, on awakening, carefully note down all that he remembered of his dreams. He was totally absorbed in this activity and almost unaware of the great events taking place in the world outside. But it all seems to have been beneficial to him, for he went through a personality change, lost most of his neurotic timidity, and rid himself almost completely of his stutter.

The other great change was his decision to publish some of his writing. His first two works were printed in limited editions at his own expense and were intended for a few friends and for his own satisfaction. He had not yet decided to publish for the general public, but it was a step in that direction. *Dans les années sordides* appeared in Monaco in 1943. It is a collection of prose poems evoking the "sordid" war years that he spent in Monte Carlo, and it is based largely on the dreams that he had experienced. The poet Paul Eluard, who was a friend of Mandiargues, was amazed when he was given a copy of the work, for he had not realized that Mandiargues was writing. (Although this is Mandiargues's first published work, some earlier poems, written from 1935 onwards, appeared in *L'Age de craie* in 1961.) The second of these works published in limited editions was *Hedera ou la persistance de l'amour pendant une rêverie*, a long love poem dedicated to the surrealist painter Méret Oppenheim, which appeared in 1945. It is written in irregular verse and its author calls it "the most surreal of my poems," adding that it "springs directly from dream and rêverie."

When the war ended, Mandiargues went back to Paris, where he began publishing regularly. In 1946, a short story, "L'Etudiante," was published by Fontaine, and a volume of short stories called *Le Musée noir* by Laffont. These were no longer limited editions, but works available to a wider public. *Le Musée noir* is a collection of fantastic tales in which the cruel, the erotic, and dream are mingled in a way that shows Mandiargues already at the height of his powers. Each story is a tableau, an exhibit in a "black museum," and, although all are in what is already a "typical" Mandiargues vein, each one has a slightly different atmosphere. "Le Sang de l'agneau" is a tale of blood, violence, and lost virginity; "Le passage Pommeraye" one of mystery and horror; "L'Homme du parc Monceau" an elaborate allegory of sexual intercourse and of the urges inside man; "Mouton noir" another tale of blood; "Le Tombeau d'Aubrey Beardsley" baroque, complex, and rather puzzling; "Le Pont" the haunting tale of a magical forest.

Unfortunately, as Mandiargues points out, the years immediately after the war were not propitious ones for this kind of fantasy. It was a time when existentialist philosophy dominated the French literary scene and when literature had to be "serious" and politically committed. He describes this philosophy as "a pseudo-philosophy, as mediocre as it was arrogant" and condemns its practitioners as having no concern for style and language. To show an interest in style was to be branded by them as "an aesthete and behind the times." While these comments are excessively harsh to a movement which contributed a new and vital element to French literature and thought, one can sympathize with Mandiargues's sense of frustration. It must indeed have been galling, after years of secret preparation and perfection of one's art, to be told that style was unimportant and that one was behind the times.

But Mandiargues was not discouraged. In 1951, he published *Soleil des loups*, a collection of six stories combining his now familiar ingredients of fantasy and cruelty. They are all set under the sign and the influence of the moon, a cold, unearthly presence that broods over the strange destiny of Mandiargues's characters. In the early 1950s Marcel Arland said that this volume "sparkles and shimmers," and that the stories in it are ones "where surrealism is combined with the rarest romantic vein."[5] Comparisons were made between Mandiargues and Bosch, Mérimée, Salvador Dali, and Nodier, and it clearly impressed the critics, for it was awarded the *Prix des critiques* for 1951.[6] This was followed in 1953 by his first novel, *Marbre*, a diffuse, rather disjointed work divided into six almost distinct parts. Although he does not yet seem to be entirely at home with the novel form, this marks an important step toward the major novels that were to come later. His delight in geometry, ceremonial settings, and strange rituals finds some of its most sustained expression in *Marbre*, set in an Italy that Roger Nimier calls "partly the work of Mediterranean gods, partly the work of Leonardo da Vinci, Max Ernst, Salvador Dali, and Léonor Fini."[7]

Three years later, Mandiargues proved himself the master of the short novel form with the publication of one of his most charming tales, *Le Lis de mer*. Set in a Mediterranean world of sun, sea, and sensual enjoyment of nature, it depicts a character's unusual sensitivity to the natural world. It contains gripping scenes of sexual initiation, ritual, and eroticism, and it is full of mythical allusions. *Le Lis de mer* plunges us into a world where "eroticism joins the poetry of the earth, the sea, and the sky."[8] Although it is a novel in which unlikely things may happen at any time and where "two worlds interpenetrate and coexist, where anything becomes possible,"[9] it is written in a style that makes it "in its strict realism, the most beautiful of his books."[10]

During these years, Mandiargues had also acquired a circle of friends who appreciated him and his work: Jean Paulhan, André Breton, Benjamin Péret, Julien Gracq, Jacques Audiberti, Francis Ponge, Georges Limbour, Jean Dubuffet, Germaine Richier, René de Solier, and

Georges Lambrichs. Many of these names are linked with surrealism, a movement that he had discovered long before this, in 1926 or 1927, when he began to visit José Corti's bookstore in Paris. Although the movement had suffered an eclipse during the war, when Breton was exiled in the United States, it revived somewhat on his return. It never achieved the vitality and importance that it had once known, but it did attract a number of new and talented adherents. In 1946, Mandiargues became associated with what he calls in *Le Désordre de la mémoire* this "second age of surrealism".

When literary circles were dominated by the existentialists and their disapproval of "frivolous" literature, surrealism obviously offered a more congenial atmosphere, where dreams, fantasy, and sheer imagination were appreciated. It cannot be said that he acually "joined" the surrealists, and he himself says that "I only had one foot in the group." Yet he was certainly associated with them for some years. This did not last, however, for he refused to follow slavishly the dictates of André Breton. "Unlike many surrealists," he says, "who sought only to look through the boss's spectacles and whose vision was distorted by frequent changes of lenses, I gave way several times to the need to 'put my foot in it.'" The spirit of independence and revolt, which Mandiargues considers to be "eminently surrealist," did not always endear him to Breton. He sees the latter's desire to impose his will on the other surrealists as a kind of spiritual exercise intended to test them, and he argues that Breton disliked excessive servility as much as insubordination. He declines to condemn Breton and angrily rejects the title of "Pope of Surrealism" that some critics have given this poet. Nevertheless, his own attitude of independence was bound to cause friction with the leader of the group.

The first coolness between the two came when Mandiargues published a study of René de Solier in which he praised this writer for his love of literature. Breton and his followers always made a distinction between "literature" and "poetry," and they despised mere "literature" as a vulgar, commercial product. Mandiargues, on the other hand, describes much surrealist work as "literature," and believes that there is nothing to be ashamed of in that. The two also disagreed over the importance of Mallarmé, whom Breton tended to dismiss as being of minor importance, while Mandiargues, as he says in *Le Désordre de la mémoire*, has always placed him "above all others in that old and new and always beloved French literature." Breton argued too that Ronsard, Rabelais, and Hoffmann were not of great importance, while Mandiargues esteems them highly. Consequently, although there is no definite point at which Mandiargues actually broke with the group, he began to move away from them. Today, he no longer counts himself as one of them, but he has never ceased to praise the surrealists.

Meanwhile there had been another important event in his life.

He describes in *Bona l'amour et la peinture* how, in October 1947, he met Bona Tibertelli, the niece of the Italian painter Filippo de Pisis, and an artist in her own right. Filippo de Pisis, who was already a good friend of his, had asked him to arrange accommodation for him and his niece during a visit to Paris. As Mandiargues was walking to the hotel to greet them, a phrase kept going through his mind: "There are beautiful October days in Paris." He remembers little of that first meeting, except being struck by the beauty of Bona's face, and especially of her eyes. She became the great love of his life, and he married her in Modena on 2 February 1950. He writes: "Bona is for me, more than anything else, the woman I love, and . . . she is the inspiration for most of my poems." The book *Bona l'amour et la peinture* was written as an account of her painting, but also as an expression of his love for her. Although they were separated in 1960, they later came together again. On 24 July 1967 Bona gave birth to their daughter, whom they named Sibylle.

The late 1950s and the 1960s also saw the publication of more works of fiction. *Feu de braise* (1959) contains seven stories, four of which ("Feu de braise," "Miroir morne," "Le Nu parmi les cercueils," and "L'Enfantillage") are based on dreams or reverie. Two others ("Le Diamant" and "Les Pierreuses") use the mineral world as the basis for the characters' unusual and terrifying experiences. "Le Diamant" is a particularly fine story, a complex mesh of allusions to myth and alchemy in which we observe a character suddenly changing size—an element of fantasy that finds its way into later stories. This work was another critical success and was awarded the *Prix de la nouvelle*. In 1963 he published his third novel, *La Motocyclette*, in which he deals much more with the "real" world than in his previous fiction. It describes a woman's journey on a motorcycle along fast highways and through actual towns. Yet the realism is a springboard to dream and imagination. When it was published, one critic wrote à propos of it that "the unusual can take on the perspective of the fantastic while also occasionally retaining the appearance of the familiar."[11] The motorcycle of the title becomes an unleashed, elemental spirit, and, as another critic said, "Mandiargues achieves an impressive sensuous evocation of riding the motorcycle."[12] There is a very strong erotic flavor to the work, and several scenes of cruel, almost sadistic sexual excess. It was mentioned as a possible winner of one of the annual literary prizes, but was not successful.[13] It was, however, made into a film entitled *Naked Under Leather* by Jack Cardiff.

In *Porte dévergondée* (1965), Mandiargues sets out deliberately to create a special world, one which, he points out in his preface, demands that the reader make an effort to adapt himself. It consists of four stories with extraordinary baroque décors that seem to dominate the characters and affect their behavior: a curious hotel room ("Sabine"), an elaborate dream world ("La Grotte"), a most unusual theatre ("Le Théâtre de Pornopapas"), and a strange old house ("Le Fils de rat"). The explicit sexual content of the first three tales shows, as Mandiargues admits in the preface, an obvious desire to shock.

La Marge (1967) is Mandiargues's most important novel, a major work in which he shows himself capable of treating his usual themes in a sustained manner and on a wider scale than previously. It is particularly interesting (as will be seen later) for its use of time, but it also contains the familiar mixture of fantasy, mythical references, dreamlike sequences, and eroticism. The setting is rather more "sordid" than usual—the prostitutes' quarter of Barcelona, which is described in realistic detail. This realism of style led one critic to refer to the novel's "slow and minutely developed detail, its delectable precision,"[14] but the precision does not stifle the author's fantasy. Another reviewer rightly called it a "work of delicate imaginative power."[15] This volume is a worthy successor to his previous ones, a notable climax to years of writing, and it finally brought him the recognition that his work deserved: the Goncourt Prize for 1967. This was not just a sign of critical approval, but also ensured it a wider public than his works had hitherto commanded.

He still found time, while writing these works, for another favorite activity: traveling. He has always spent as much of his time as possible in Italy, but he has traveled in several other European countries too. In 1958, he took a six-month trip to Mexico, and he went to Cuba in 1968 to attend a congress of writers friendly to that country. The second of these journeys was obviously undertaken out of a sense of solidarity with Castro and his government. Mandiargues has, more than once, expressed apparently left-wing opinions and has said in *Le Désordre de la mémoire*: "I have a lot of sympathy for the communists, especially French and Italian communists, who seem to me the only party men resolved to struggle against social injustice and to improve as best they can men's situation, to change life, as the surrealists used to say." Speaking in 1975, when *Le Désordre de la mémoire* was published, he described the régimes of Mao in China, of Boumedienne in Algeria and of Castro in Cuba as "morally exemplary," while he condemned the United States, then engaged in a war in Vietnam, as "the champion of criminality in the world today."

None of these statements should be taken to mean that Mandiargues is, or ever has been, a communist. In fact, before the Second World War, he even had a certain sympathy for Italian fascism. He now describes himself as "apolitical" and as having "strong anarchist tendencies."[16] He has never voted, and he has always refused to obtain the *carte d'électeur* needed in order to vote in France. His statements on political matters are moral ones, expressing his reactions to events of the day. He sided with the communists at the time of French involvement in Indochina and in Algeria because they were the only ones in France to oppose these colonial wars. For the same reason, he signed, in 1960, the "Manifesto of the Hundred and One"—a protest by writers and intellectuals against the war in Algeria. His anti-Americanism was a response to American activities in Vietnam, and he denies being anti-American today. On the contrary, in view of recent events in Cambodia, Vietnam, and Afghanistan, he now professes a strong anti-communism. He even regrets Castro's current orientation, while still admitting to a certain sympathy for a man whom he describes as "a marvelous intellectual whom I met in Havana" in 1968.

As Mandiargues's admission of anarchist tendencies would suggest, he is less of a political revolutionary than an admirer of revolt and of the anti-bourgeois spirit. Like André Breton, he saw communism at specific times as a means of righting certain wrongs, and especially as a form of revolt against attitudes and ways of life that he despises. It is the idea of revolt rather than of revolution that animates his work and many of his opinions. He admits in *Le Désordre de la mémoire* that it is "to this spirit of revolt . . . that I owe the great love of the avant-garde that I have always maintained." It is this same anti-conformism which led him to refuse the *Légion d'honneur* and to say that he would never wish to belong to the French Academy.

Mandiargues's main concerns have always been literary and artistic rather than political. In the 1970s, two other works of fiction were published by him. *Mascarets* (1971) is a collection of eight short stories, all strongly erotic in nature. They are built around a variety of situations, most of them involving fairly "normal" sex, but also oral sex ("La Marée"), and bestiality ("Adive"). "La Marée" is a particularly interesting tale, written at the request of André Breton for inclusion in the catalog of an exhibition on eroticism organized by the surrealists in 1959. It is one of the best examples of how Mandiargues links sexual activity to a certain attitude toward the natural world, and it has also been made into a film by the Polish director Borowczyk.[17] One story ("La Révélation") links sex explicitly and in a rather grisly way to death. Three others ("Le Marronnier," "Les Formes charnelles," and "Le Triangle ambigu") set out to destroy our logical, rationalistic attitudes about reality by depicting situations in which the nature of time is questioned and dream mingles with "real" events. He creates what a reviewer called a world "where our old certainties totter and perspectives are changed."[18] The setting of "La Marée" and "Mascarets" is the beach and cliffs of Normandy that he has loved since his childhood. The title of the volume, and of the last story in it, refers to a current that flows up from a river's mouth as the tide changes. But *mascaret* is also slang for ejaculation, and it neatly conveys the sexual undercurrent in all the stories. One critic exclaimed: "What music in the language, the very music of the sea," and another called *Mascarets* "a perfect illustration of baroque art."[19]

His most recent work of fiction is another collection of short stories called *Sous la lame* (1976). The six pieces in this volume are tales of sadism, blood, and violence, as the title of the work suggests. One of them, "Mil neuf cent trente-trois," is dedicated to the "shades of Mishima," a writer who fascinated Mandiargues by his cruelty and sadism and whose work, *Madame de Sade*, he has translated into French. These tales are also an exploration of the hidden depths of man's mind, of the dark impulses that lie within us, and a plea that we accept them as essential parts of our nature. In 1979, he also published under his own name a work that had appeared in 1953 under the assumed name of Paul Morion. *L'Anglais décrit dans le château fermé* is a series of sado-erotic incidents in an isolated castle. Clearly inspired by Sade, it is a tale of suffering, cruel tortures, and even death inflicted on a variety of not always unwilling victims for the pleasure of the two main characters.

From 1943 to the present day, Mandiargues has been continually engaged in writing and publishing. Mention has been made only of his fiction in this chapter, but he has published many other works besides. Several volumes of poetry have established his reputation as a sensitive poet combining the baroque and classical styles evident in his fiction and treating the same themes of eroticism, dream, love of nature, and delight in the marvelous. One of these volumes, *L'Ivre œil*, won the French Academy's *Grand prix de la poésie* in 1978. He has also written for the theatre, although not with great success. In 1973, his first play, *Isabella Morra*, was performed in Paris with Jean-Louis Barrault and Anny Duperey in the main roles. Mandiargues admits that most of the critics did not like or understand the play, but this did not deter him from publishing a second one in 1979: *La Nuit séculaire*. This one has not yet been performed.

As well as being a creative writer, Mandiargues is also a literary and art critic of considerable perception. He has written about many painters, from El Greco to Max Ernst, but with a definite preference for avant-garde art. His literary criticism covers what is probably an even wider field, ranging from Balzac to Breton, from *De l'amour* to *Histoire d'O*. Novalis, Hoffmann, Kleist, Jean-Paul Richter, Gide, Baudelaire, Mallarmé, the surrealists, Pascal, Voltaire, Chateaubriand, Rousseau, Nerval, Flaubert, Jarry, Claudel, Cingria, Scève, the English Elizabethan poets, Coleridge, Lautréamont, Bataille, and Nodier are but some of those whose works he has read, thought about, and assimilated. He reserves special praise and admiration for André Breton, Jean Paulhan, and Marcel Jouhandeau, writers whom he counted as friends as well as exemplars when they were alive. Finally, not the least in his affections, and a writer whose influence on him is obvious in nearly all his works, is the Marquis de Sade.

Pieyre de Mandiargues's life has been devoted above all else to art and literature. The fruit of this is a rich and varied body of critical work. But the result of his years of study and preparation is also a series of fictional works in which his own vivid imagination is expressed. These works place him in the same rank as many of those whom he has studied and praised as his masters.

2

Eros and Pan

Toute la nature est portée par un courant de passion: de l'arbre au cerf, de la racine au sanglier se tendent les vigueurs naïves.

Jacques Chessex, *Reste avec nous*

THERE ARE MANY SOURCES OF FASCINATION in Mandiargues's fiction, but not least among them is their erotic content. It is not easy to say just how he provokes erotic emotion, but women and the naked female form naturally have a central part in the process. Mandiargues, like the surrealists, sees woman as a constant source of wonder, and much of the power of his writing comes from the way in which he conveys this wonder. The delight and awe felt by the young man in *Le Lis de mer* as he contemplates the heroine whose "breasts were round and perfect, finely proportioned and superbly swelling, [whose] build was tall and graceful . . . and [whose] legs were slim with long, beautifully rounded thighs" are typical of the feelings of many male characters. One such description of a naked woman, in a story from *Feu de braise* ("Le Nu parmi les cercueils") runs for four pages.

Mandiargues believes that the female form has always been "an elemental substance" for anyone with a feeling for the marvelous.[1] He argues in *Troisième Belvédère* that woman has never failed to provoke this feeling of awe, and that primitive man depicted naked women in some of his earliest paintings in order to express his sense of almost religious marvel. As a poet, Mandiargues thinks that he is particularly sensitive to such emotion, and he has said in *Le Désordre de la mémoire:* "I am like most poets: I think that there is nothing in this world, or, at least, on the face of the earth where we walk, which has caused us so much wonder, and which will cause us so much wonder, as woman."

The erotic in Mandiargues's work does not rely entirely on the contemplation of woman's body. It contains another, more disturbing, element, for his is a cruel and sadistic eroticism of chains, bonds, blood, and torture. A young girl is raped by a Negro shepherd in a hut smelling of animal excrement, while the sheep mill around; a woman is tied up and

13

flagellated by roses before her torturer brutally possesses her; another girl is bound, beaten, and killed by her brothers in an atmosphere charged with incestuous emotion; a man submits to whipping by a prostitute wearing a large artificial phallus.[2] One whole novel, *L'Anglais décrit dans le château fermé*, is a series of tableaux depicting the sexual excesses of a group of people in an isolated château. This novel of gothic horror culminates in the murder of a baby, who is cut down the middle and torn almost in half, and in the rape of its helpless mother, who has been obliged to watch her child's death. While the narrator of the novel is filled with revulsion, the other adult participants, including the mother, are overcome by frenzied sexual pleasure.[3]

What Mandiargues describes in such scenes as these goes beyond mere *gauloiserie* or smuttiness. He has no interest in that kind of titillation of the reader, and he has written in *Le Cadran lunaire* that "everything that has been called 'dirty jokes' or (wrongly, in all probability) 'Gallic humor' is as irksome in eroticism as the midday sun to an owl." He seeks, rather, to shock the reader, for he has a definite taste for what upsets and disturbs. He has always preferred art which is, to quote his description of Dada in *Deuxième Belvédère*, "disconcerting, disrespectful, subversive, and shocking in its doctrine," and he has consistently tried to make his own work fit that description. His introduction to *Porte dévergondée* proclaims with pride: "It is the nature of these adventures or stories to shock the spectator or the listener. He is shocked in his convictions, in his most honorable feelings, in his beloved culture, in his modesty and in his tastes."

But it is a particular kind of shock that Mandiargues wants to produce in the erotic passages of his fiction. In an article from *Troisième Belvédère* called "Un puissant moteur de la littérature," he examines Georges Bataille's theories of eroticism, and, by so doing, indicates the nature of the kind of shock he seeks to provoke. He points out that, according to Bataille, the darkly disturbing emotions generated by sadistic eroticism are due to a sense of transgression. Eroticism is, as the title of the article claims, "a powerful motive force in literature" because it produces a deep sense of excitement and perturbation at breaking society's accepted norms.

In view of Mandiargues's interest in Bataille's ideas, and since they both see eroticism as a form of transgression, it is useful to apply certain other aspects of Bataille's theory to Mandiargues's work. Although Mandiargues does not mention this in his article, Bataille also points out that all societies have accepted practices for transgressing the established code. These practices are carefully regulated, and are surrounded by ritual and ceremony which make them solemn, religious occasions.

Transgression is thus controlled, and it completes rather than destroys the codes that it violates. Provision is made for the need to feel the emotion of transgression, while maintaining the code that makes the transgression possible.[4]

Eroticism in Mandiargues's fiction fits very closely what Bataille says, for the erotic scenes in his work are almost invariably accompanied by elaborate ritual. Although often cruel and bloody, they have a sacred, magic air about them. One is not witnessing cruelty and torture for their own sake, but something like a religious ceremony in which those who take part transcend their suffering or their bloody deeds. Sometimes even the sense of transgression is lost, and ideas of good and evil, right and wrong are no longer relevant, for victim and torturer both consent to the acts of cruelty. Referring to this kind of eroticism in *Le Cadran lunaire* as "black eros," Mandiargues defines it as "the boundless community where good and evil become one and where all things are rigorously equal."

Almost any of Mandiargues's fiction could provide us with examples of ritualized sexual activity. I have limited myself in this chapter mainly to three of his works, *Le Lis de mer*, *La Motocyclette*, and a short story in *Le Musée noir* called "Le Sang de l'agneau," with a brief mention of "La Marée," a story in *Mascarets*. These constitute the best and most sustained examples of the points that I wish to make, but it must be borne in mind that many other works illustrate the same points.[5]

Le Lis de mer is a short, fast-moving novel which captures the atmosphere of an isolated Mediterranean coast redolent with pagan sensuality. The heroine is a young girl called Vanina who is on holiday in Sardinia with her friend, Juliette. In the opening scene, they are basking in the sun and swimming in the sea. Vanina notices that one of the local youths is observing her closely, and, when she and her friend leave the beach, they pass close by him. Moved by a sudden impulse, she whispers a rendezvous to him. She has no idea why she does this, and is slightly shocked afterwards. Nevertheless, she does go to meet him and, as she talks to him, she issues a variety of instructions which she does not really understand and which do not seem to come from her.

Vanina is still a virgin, and she has jealously guarded her purity. But she does possess an imagination which makes her more sexually aware than Juliette, who has had more actual sexual experience. This explains to some extent Vanina's sudden willingness to meet with a strange man and to arrange further meetings with him. She has also read several erotic works, and this too helps explain her acts. What is more difficult to understand is her apparently innate sense of ritual. When she goes to the tryst, she tells the young man that he will become her lover later, but first he must come, at night, to the house where she is lodging, and he must look through the window of her room. When he does so, he sees that she has prepared a deliberately ritualistic tableau for him. She lies on her bed, naked but for a gold necklace, her hair spread out on the pillow, pale lipstick on her lips, eyelids and eyebrows darkened, face lightly powdered, with candles burning on either side of her, and a mound of white lilies at her feet. The man is naturally tempted to enter the room and avail himself of Vanina there and then. Yet even he is overawed by the atmosphere, and it only takes a small gesture from the girl to halt him. The reader shares his sense of awe and knows that this is not a scene of *gauloiserie*, but one expressly constructed to prevent any such connotation.

There is a second erotic scene which is even more moving. Vanina goes again to meet the man, this time with the intention of giving herself to him. She insists, however, that he follow a ritual which she herself dictates "in its tiniest details, like a ballet contrived for a king and queen." He has to seize her, bind her hands, and brutally take her virginity from her. But he must do so with a slow and almost reverent deliberation. The place chosen for this pagan ceremony is a kind of natural arena in the woods, an area free from all growth and contaminatiion and surrounded by a profusion of lilies that emit a heady perfume. Vanina prepares herself psychologically and physically well in advance. She selects the simplest clothes and rejects all jewelry and ornaments, and the very simplicity of her dress adds to the solemnity of the occasion. We are witnessing, in this scene, something more than a chance sexual encounter.

Before we inquire further into the true significance of this erotic incident, it is instructive to examine another of Mandiargues's novels, *La Motocyclette*. This is a longer, more complex work than *Le Lis de mer*, which is a straightforward tale narrated in chronological order and with one or two flashbacks. *La Motocyclette* combines a web of symbolic references with a narrative technique that shifts constantly in time. It tells how Rebecca Nul leaves her sleeping husband early one morning and sets out on her motorcycle to meet her lover. She travels from the border town in France, where her husband is a lycée teacher, to the German town where her lover, Daniel, lives. As she travels, her mind ranges back in time, recalling past journeys to her lover and other occasions when she met him. The technique is rather similar to the *nouveau roman* in that it attempts to capture lived time, or time as Rebecca experiences it. Like Butor's *La Modification*, it uses the framework of a journey during which landmarks and familiar sights provoke memories of previous journeys. This is a more complicated and deliberately thought-out technique than was used in the earlier novel. The setting too is very different, for it is resolutely "realistic," with references to actual places, explanations of how motorcycles function, descriptions of roads, pedestrians, other vehicles, towns and rivers, and a detailed route map of the journey. *Le Lis de mer*, on the other hand, although set in Sardinia, could really take place in any sunny, hot land, and has a vague, mythical atmosphere.

Where the two novels do coincide is in their erotic content. In *La Motocyclette* Rebecca's mind dwells insistently on the times when she has met Daniel and on her sexual adventures with him. One such memory is startlingly similar to Vanina's experience in its ritualistic semireligious nature. On this particular occasion she met her lover in a Turkish bath and had to gain entrance to a private room at the very heart of the establishment—a kind of inner sanctum where the ritual was to take place. Daniel tied the naked girl to a pipe in the wall, then, after observing her intently for some time, he slowly flagellated her with a bunch of roses. Then he untied her scratched and bleeding body and "among the petals from the roses with which she had been beaten, Daniel . . . had seized her with a brutality which she had never before experienced."

This scene and the erotic ones from *Le Lis de mer* constitute a ritual sacrifice, and the women involved are sacrificial victims. In *Le Lis de mer* Vanina submissively offers herself, bound and naked, to the man, who becomes a practitioner of some obscure religious rite. In Rebecca's case, there are even allusions to Christ, the most celebrated of all sacrificial victims. The beating with roses recalls the flagellation of Christ, and the thorns on the roses remind us of the crown of thorns put on him by the Roman soldiers. Mandiargues even describes Rebecca's trussed body as forming "an oblique cross." On another occasion in *La Motocyclette*, Daniel possesses her sexually in a forest, holding her arms outstretched, as though in crucifixion, against a tree trunk. There is, in this scene, a veiled allusion to the resurrection, for Rebecca is compared to a dead woman as she lies under her lover, and, when he has finished, "he helped the dead girl to rise up." A more pagan sacrificial rite is brought to mind in yet another scene where Daniel swiftly pulls down the zipper on Rebecca's motorcyclists' garment "as though it had been sliced in two by a knife blade," reminding one of the sacrificial animal cut open by a priest—especially since, as we shall see later, Rebecca is more than once compared to an animal. Rebecca herself realizes the role she is playing, for she compares herself to "a prisoner of the Indians of New Spain, bound and waiting at the summit of a pyramid for the glorious moment when her breast would be opened by the stroke of an obsidian stone knife."[6]

As befits sacrificial offerings, both women undergo a ritual preparation before the actual ceremony. In *Le Lis de mer* Vanina washes her feet and her body, and, as she approaches the appointed spot, she wades through a stream to cleanse her feet again. She eats frugally before setting off to meet the man, undertaking something like a ritual fast; she removes her shoes after setting out, as though walking on hallowed ground. Rebecca too, on the occasion when she meets her lover in the Turkish bath, bathes herself before he arrives.[7]

In these mysterious ceremonies, the man plays the role of a priest. There are, indeed, several indications in *La Motocyclette* that Rebecca sees Daniel in a distinctly religious light. She remembers him as having, on one occasion, "the appearance of a mad preacher" and on another as looking like a "prophet or a saint." When he comes to her in the Turkish bath, he is dressed in a white robe which gives him "his usual air of being the priest of some strange religion." As he bends over her, the light in the room seems to turn the robe crimson, like the crimson or purple ones worn by priest kings.

Every detail of the typical religious sacrifice is present, even the fact that, as in most such ceremonies, the victims are willing ones. In *Le Lis de mer* Vanina longs from the secret depths of her being to be a sacrifice. She tells her companion that she envies the Polynesian girls who, when they first came in contact with Europeans, would swim out to their ships to be manhandled, taken by the sailors, and thrown back in the sea. When she does become a sacrifice, she gives herself "body and spirit to the troubling joy of feeling herself a weak, vanquished creature, seized, bound, and thrown to the ground." Rebecca too offers herself freely as a victim. She eagerly parts from her timid husband, a mild-mannered school teacher who cannot even control his pupils, and rides off, full of erotic daydreams of her cruel, demanding lover who easily bends her to his will.

Before leaving the question of eroticism as sacrifice in Mandiargues's work, reference should be made to a story from *Le Musée noir* in which the heroine is both sacrifice and sacrificer. "Le Sang de l'agneau" is one of Mandiargues's most disturbing tales of sudden, violent emotion springing from the hidden depths of characters who are pushed to ritualized sadism and murder. The heroine, Marceline Caïn, is a young girl on the threshold of womanhood. Her mother decides that Marceline must stop behaving like a child, and buys her new, women's clothes to mark her change in status. While they are in town buying the clothes, Marceline's father kills her pet rabbit and the servant serves it up that evening. The pet, which was her link to childhood, becomes, as it were, a sacrifice to mark Marceline's passage into womanhood. Her parents watch with sadistic glee as she unknowingly eats the rabbit; then they take great pleasure in revealing to her what she has done. Later that night, she leaves the house, goes to a nearby tavern, and is taken by a Negro shepherd to his hut, where he rapes her. Realizing that he has been the instrument in some dark ritual which he cannot understand, and awed by the act he has committed, he hangs himself before Marceline's fascinated eyes. She refuses to cut him down when, at the last moment, he seems to regret his act. Instead, she takes his knife home and butchers her sleeping parents.

Marceline also is a sacrificial lamb. In fact, the Negro tells her: "You are a pretty, wooly lamb in the hands of the black butcher." Overcome by the heady, animal smell of the sheep who press around, Marceline feels as though she has become one of them, and, when the Negro seizes her, "she hears rising in her mouth a real bleating which retains no trace of her girl's voice." The sheep, on hearing this, break out of their pen and frenziedly press even closer "still bleating as though for a little lamb being butchered." The Negro, at this point, plays the role of sacrificer, and Marceline is not unwilling in her role as victim. She admits that "she must have her share in the responsibility for everything that took place."

But Marceline plays a double role. When she recovers from the rape, she realizes that the shepherd's hands are bound behind his back. Since he could not have done this himself, we have to conclude that Marceline did it while still semiconscious. Like her biblical namesake, Marceline Caïn now becomes the sacrificer. Not only does she decline to save the shepherd, she sacrifices her own parents with the Negro's knife—on the handle of which is carved a ram.

Marceline's rape is like some grim, pagan initiation rite. Marceline is passing the frontier from girlhood to womanhood, a passage accompanied by the spilled blood of her virginity. Rebecca, in her first encounter with Daniel, and Vanina when she couples with the young man, also sacrifice their virginity. In these three stories, as in several others,[8] Mandiargues shows a fascinated interest in this critical moment in a woman's life, and in *Le Désordre de la mémoire* he admits to "a mania . . . for attributing so much importance to a woman's defloration." He points out in his preface to *Le Musée noir*, that men have always felt a certain fear and mystery in the spilled blood of virginity, and he argues that this is because it represents a symbolic murder of the girl's parents, who are replaced as the dominating force in her life. In primitive societies, this severing of parental influence is conveyed symbolically in puberty rites. "Le Sang de l'agneau" shows the symbolic becoming real when Marceline actually does kill her parents. Much of the horror of this story comes from the sudden revelation of the reality that lurks behind such ceremonies.

Yet, strangely enough, all three of these women retain a kind of innocence and purity. Although Rebecca many times complies with Daniel's lascivious will, and although she relishes these moments in her mind, she stays an inexplicably pure figure; Marceline's act of murder is not one of vengeful hate which would stain her, but something which seems to redress a certain balance in the nature of things; Vanina's deliberate gift of herself, and all the elaborate arrangements she makes to give this gift, do not alter her essential innocence. The fact is that these characters act as though their decisions are made for them, as though they are possessed by forces outside them which take over their minds. They are able to plan rituals and to give themselves as willing victims because their wills are not entirely their own. They remain innocent because they are merely instruments.

It is as though some force propels Rebecca toward Daniel in *La Motocyclette*. She is awakened from her sleep by a dream in which she is lying in the topmost branches of a tree while birds fly around her. Moved in a way which she cannot understand, she leaves her home and sets out towards Daniel. Her journey is thus linked from its very beginning to a mysterious power, for dreams have been regarded by man from the earliest times as the means by which forces outside of him make themselves known. The birds which figure in the dream are also important, since man has often used the entrails of sacrificed birds and the patterns of their flight as a way of divining the will of the forces which govern his life. An unknown power pushes Rebecca on, and, as she accelerates on her motorcycle, "it seems as though a powerful hand hurls her forward faster than ever." She is reduced to nothing, emptied of her own being, and this is indicated by her very name: Rebecca Nul.[9] (She was once called Rebecca Res, which suggests that she was something before this force took her over.)

In *Le Lis de mer* Vanina is no less the instrument of powerful influences, and it is obviously these which prompt her to arrange the meeting with a stranger. When she looks back on this, in a moment of calm and lucidity, she is surprised that she was so bold. When she explains to the man the ritual he must follow, it seems again that something else is speaking through her, and she produces "a flood of words, which were nevertheless ordered, while her thoughts ran after the words without her understanding anything that was happening." In "Le Sang de l'agneau" Marceline too, when she runs off and finds the shepherd and when she kills her parents, is obeying a will other than her own. She is described as a "conscious automaton" and a "lucid sleepwalker," and she is so detached from her acts that she has the impression of standing at a distance and observing herself.

One has to conclude that the forces taking possession of Mandiargues's women come from outside of them. They are, in fact, situated in the surrounding world, and especially in the natural world. Rebecca, Vanina, and Marceline have a special relationship with nature, and seem to sense a life within it which is not perceptible to most people. This is evident in the delight that Vanina takes in swimming and basking in the

sun, for it goes beyond the usual tourists' pleasure in beaches and pictur-
esque scenery. She senses something mysterious that moves in the sun,
the sea, and the vegetation, and, as she walks in the wood, it is as though
the ground beneath her is breathing. She is drawn particularly to the lilies
growing on the shore, and she experiences a deeply sensual pleasure in
breathing their strangely intoxicating perfume. Marceline, for her part,
feels these forces in the night and the moonlit sky rather than in the
daylight world. Both of them, despite their innocence, are wise to an
elemental sensuality in the world in which they live.

Throughout *La Motocyclette* Rebecca's close intimacy with nature is built up by means of a whole series of metaphors which compare
her to parts of the natural world. Her husband refers to her endearingly as
a "squirrel" and a "bird"; her motorcyclists' outfit is compared to an animal
skin; she thinks of herself at one point as being like a goat; and, as she
looks at her naked body in a mirror, she thinks that "her nakedness made
her like leaves picked up in the undergrowth in autumn." When she
walks among the trees, she feels an intense emotion communicated by the
trembling leaves and the wind in the branches. Her husband tells her that
what she feels at such times is "a kind of pulsation or breathing of living
nature that man discovered with a mixture of respect and fear."

There is something erotic in the way in which Vanina and Rebecca react to the world around them. Mandiargues establishes in his
fiction a direct link between the erotic and the forces of nature, and he has
said in *Le Désordre de la mémoire:* "The natural fruit of participation in
the outside world is love." It is, in fact, during the erotic scenes in his
work that his characters feel most intensely the hidden powers in the
world surrounding them. When the heroine of *Le Lis de mer* is possessed
by the man in the forest she is also possessed by the forces of creation
itself. Her consciousness suddenly expands to encompass the whole
world, and she seems to commune with the night sky, the moon, and the
lilies growing close by. Her hair mingles with the sandy soil, and her
breasts seem to draw life from the moonlight, until she feels "a sort of
essential analogy or relationship between them and these heavy flowers
and the moon." The sound of the sea accompanies their union, and "she
felt, at last, as she had so often desired, that she was 'communicating with
the whole of nature.'"

Rebecca's experience of the world in *La Motocyclette* is almost
identical. Just before her first union with Daniel, she lies in her hotel
room already feeling as though she is part of nature—in this case, the
mineral world. She has the impression that she is lying at the center of a
gem, and her ring, which bears a large beryl, glitters supernaturally in
the moonlight.[10] When Daniel arrives and they begin to make love, "she
committed her body and her consciousness to violence and to the night

as, in other seasons, she had committed them to the sun and the clear water." The snow falling outside the window seems to enter the room and envelop her, until she is actually part of it. On a later occasion, when she has sexual relations with Daniel in a wood, her consciousness fixes on some icicles nearby, and the snow once again seems to take over her whole being, so that she is "so scattered in it all that she was no longer at all certain of existing as a distinct person."

In "Le Sang de l'agneau," the forces with which the heroine achieves contact show themselves through the animal world. At the beginning of the story, we see Marceline playing with her pet rabbit, allowing it to run over her naked breasts while she kisses and caresses it. The pleasure which she derives from this is manifestly erotic, yet it remains innocent, for Marceline seems unaware of its true nature. The death of the rabbit represents the death of this innocence, and the powers which she senses around her are now darker, more dangerous ones. They are explicitly linked to the night, for, when she sets out towards the shepherd, a cold, deathly pale moon shines on her, and "everywhere could be felt the larval world of beings which sleep when the earth is in sunlight and which move in the darkness." The shepherd, because of his color and his somewhat bestial appearance, incarnates these black forces. When she enters his hut, she is overcome by the odor of sheep, which is described as "of all the thousands of animal smells in the world . . . the most openly bestial and disturbing." The Negro places her on the back of a sheep, and, slowly, she is filled with a sense of well-being and is "transformed into an animal among all the other snorting, bleating, munching animals dropping their dung all around her." When the Negro rapes her, she has become so much a part of the animal world that she is no longer able to react as a human being, and the only sound she can produce is an animal-like bleating.[11]

The magic, elemental, and often dangerous powers released in these moments of erotic ecstasy, the same powers that guide the heroines to their destined encounter with the male, are inherent in the world. They are the life forces themselves since they flow into the characters at the time of sexual union—an act which is also a manifestation of the life force. Because they are contained especially in the natural world, Mandiargues refers to them as "panic" forces, a reference to the god Pan, who, in ancient myth, incarnated the powers of creation hidden in nature. Mandiargues makes it clear that it is this force which he tries to depict in the erotic scenes in his fiction. Writing of his goal in "Le Sang de l'agneau," he says in Le Désordre de la mémoire: "I tried to give form to the mysteries of bestiality, the complicity of fleece and blood, where is to be found the obscure meaning of sacrifice, and I believe that, this time, I achieved a really convincing illustration of that old panic magic which is in some ways the prompter in my theatre."

For Mandiargues, the world is a living thing, full of unseen powers, and, since the time when his old nurse taught him to love that world, he has been aware of the "panic" power within it. In moments of erotic pleasure, his characters are able to forget their individual identity and commune directly with the living world. It is as though the life force inside them links them directly to the same force in the outside world. In fact, in *Bona l'amour et la peinture*, he defines "panic inspiration" as "the use of the dark forces of nature and the deep energy of the unconscious, awareness of animality, complicity with the growth of vegetable matter, and even with the nervous energy of the mineral world."

Mandiargues believes that certain sites, certain special parts of the world are particularly imbued with "panic" energy. In *Deuxième Belvédère* he writes of the old Mayan city of Palenque, in Mexico, which seems to have blended so much with the surrounding forest that the life within the trees and bushes breathes through the ruins. Another such place is Bomarzo, in Italy, which he describes in *Le Belvédère*. This site contains a series of enormous statues, one of which particularly attracts Mandiargues's attention. It represents a giant tearing a child apart, and, because of the "dark beauty" of its face, the mixture of brutality and erotic pleasure expressed in its traits, and the fact that it is so overgrown by vegetation as to be almost a part of the natural world, it seems that nature is communicating some cruel sexual emotion through this statue. The giant captures perfectly the moment of "panic" communion, as do so many scenes in Mandiargues's fiction. He could be commenting on his own work when he says that this statue is an attempt to give "concrete representation to a certain frenzy of the senses and the mind which has sometimes taken control of man and to which can be applied the word *panic*."

It becomes apparent now why Mandiargues surrounds the erotic scenes in his fiction with ceremonial detail and an atmosphere of religious awe. He is depicting, not just a ritual transgression of the accepted norms, as Bataille's theory suggests, although there is clearly something of that involved. It is not just the conjunction of two human beings either. It is an experience that transcends individuals, and its mysterious, dreadful nature demands a religious setting. The individuals involved are merely caught up in a cosmic event which sweeps them along. They have no will of their own, and this is especially true of the men, who are simply the instruments through which obscure powers flow. Like priests in any ceremony, they are the vessels of other forces. For Vanina in *Le Lis de mer*, her lover is "part of great, living nature, in the same way as the trees and the reeds." In her mind, he is not an individual, but is "mingled with the night," and, when she gives herself to him, "he consecrated her in some way to the powers of the night that a lover incarnated." For the heroine of *La Motocyclette*, Daniel is often a mere instrument of other powers too. She thinks of him as a tree which has been struck by lightning, and, in ancient myth, the tree is the symbol of the center of creation through which the life forces flow.[12] Lightning too is an obvious symbol of these forces. In Marceline's case, the shepherd is an instrument whose role is soon over, and with whom she dispenses once his task is finished.

At this point, mention should be made of a story in *Mascarets* which serves both as a complement and a contrast to the ones so far examined. In "La Marée" the same communion with "panic" forces may be seen, but this time it is the man who communes, while the woman serves as an instrument.[13] It tells how a young man takes his girl cousin to an isolated part of the beach, and obliges her to fellate him. The girl is rather like Vanina in her provocative and sexually aware innocence, and she willingly does her cousin's bidding. She too is depicted rather as a sacrificial lamb, and the man addresses her as "dear little she-lamb." Again, a somewhat religious atmosphere is maintained, for the man tells the girl that she must banish all frivolity from her thoughts. "I shall need meditation during the operation, and you too will meditate," he tells her.

Once the "operation" begins, the two of them rock gently to and fro, seeming to vibrate in unison with the waves as they lap the shore. The sea here represents the essential movement of the universe, and the young man talks all the while about the ebb and flow of the tides and the influence of the moon on them. The sea also has deeply sexual connotations for Mandiargues, who associates the seashore, the smell of salt winds and of seaweed with sex. Thinking back in *Le Désordre de la mémoire* to the days when he roamed the seashore, and when he learned to love the world around him, he says: "In my first solitude, before the war, and well before the advent of the hippie movement, I had made a kind of secret religion of love, and I am not unaware that its most early origin is connected with the movement of the tides at the time of the full moon, and especially of the new moon."[14]

The man in "La Marée" feels more and more that there is a current passing to him from the world outside. He says: "Never had I succeeded in finding myself in such firm and intimate communication with nature; I felt flowing within me the great vital current which flows among the planets and which goes perhaps as far as the most distant stars; I was participating in some way in the breathing of the universe." As his sexual climax approaches, he feels "so mingled with the elemental substance that it seemed as though the tide was rising in me as it was in all the world around." Naturally, the climax finally comes at the exact moment of high tide, as though both he and the world reach some magic point at which they become one.

The narrator of "La Marée," Rebecca Nul, Vanina, and Marceline Caïn are just some of Mandiargues's characters who, through erotic experience, achieve this sense of identity with something deep and dark in the world. Eroticism and "panic" communion are the cornerstones of his work, and they provide it with much of its mystery and enchantment. They lie at the heart of his fiction and of his poetry. The following lines from one of his poems sum up his concept of "panic" eroticism (lines which I have left in the original as they lose their power in translation):

> En écho de notre caresse
> La mer faisait un bruit de sexe
> Et nous connûmes soudain
> Que nous étions mis en commun
> Avec la cendre et la semence
> De tout ce qui fut ou sera
> Dans les infinités sombres[15]

Many other modern writers have included a strong erotic compo-
nent in their work, but few link it, as Mandiargues does, to love of the outside world. Writers such as Malraux, Drieu La Rochelle, Sartre, and even Proust see eroticism as an attempt by the individual to break out of his solitude and achieve some relationship with another being. For Man-
diargues, it is more important to break our isolation from the world around us, and it is man's place in that world which interests him. He believes that much of the literature, especially existentialist literature, which talks of man's isolation from his fellows, misses the point. He asks in *Deuxième Belvédère:* "Have the professors (profiteers) of philosophy ever looked at nature? Do they not know that the writer who is also worthy of the name of poet, like the artist, even when in solitude, is in perpetual communication with the animal, the vegetable, and the mineral as much as with the human, and that the earth, air, water, and fire never cease to keep him company?" The writers and artists whom he appreciates and praises are those who, in his opinion, have seen this point: Max Ernst, Dubuffet, Toledo, Germaine Richier, Baudelaire, and the romantics.[16] He even says in *Le Belvédère* that any work of art must approach the question of man's place in nature and that the "relationships between the work of art and nature . . . are never negligible, even if they only exist as rupture or refusal." Whether or not this is true of art in general is not our concern, but it is clearly true of Mandiargues's own work.

3

Eros and Thanatos

"L'érotisme a, d'une manière fondamentale, le sens de la mort."
Georges Bataille, *L'Erotisme*

BEHIND THE LIGHTHEARTED FANTASY of Pieyre de Mandiargues's fiction is a complex and often paradoxical view of life. The erotic component of his work is a vital part of that view, and, although we have already examined in some detail the theme of eroticism, it has other ramifications that have not yet even been touched on. A convenient way of approaching them is through his treatment of time. In order to do this, we must broaden our scope beyond the three or four representative works studied in the previous chapter and include his first novel, *Marbre*, what is probably his major novel, *La Marge*, and several short stories.

Since Proust, time has been a constant preoccupation of French novelists. This is particularly true of the *nouveau roman*, which tries to convey the chaos of lived experience as it is perceived by the human consciousness. Time is a vital part of that experience, and writers of the *nouveau roman* try to capture it as it appears to the consciousness. This frequently results in the loss of traditional distinctions between past, present, and future since these are all lived *now* in the human mind. In *La Motocyclette*, Mandiargues attempts something similar, for, although the novel extends over a definite period of hours, Rebecca's mind ranges freely in time. We share with her certain experiences that she has in the present, the immediate past (the house and husband she has just left), the distant past (her meetings with Daniel since her marriage), the more distant past (her life in Switzerland before she married), and the future (anticipation of her arrival at her lover's home in Heidelberg). These experiences, memories, and anticipations are lived by us as and when they occur in Rebecca's mind. It is always clear, however, whether we are reading of past, present, or future events, for Mandiargues uses the appropriate tenses to convey this information.

Yet, although we are generally aware of the chronology of the novel, the author sometimes causes a temporary suspension of time.

26

Rebecca has left her watch behind and has no precise idea of what the time is at any given moment. Hence, despite the detailed description of places which locates her spatially in an accurate and verifiable way, she is situated temporally in only the vaguest way. *Le Lis de mer*, although it follows a broadly chronological narration, also gives the impression of existing outside of temporal categories. Vanina lies on the beach, having taken off her watch, and the sun beating down on her seems to "take away all notion of time." The dreamlike rituals to which both she and Rebecca submit themselves add to this sense of timelessness.

Two of Mandiargues's short stories contain within them periods which are deliberately depicted as beyond temporal flow. In *Le Musée noir* is an eerie tale called "Le passage Pommeraye," which begins with a man wandering around Nantes on 14 July. (Nantes was described by André Breton as "perhaps, together with Paris, the only city in France where I have the feeling that something worthwhile could happen to me."[1]) The man notices a covered street to which he feels strangely drawn. When he enters it, he finds himself in a new, mysterious world of half light where shop windows display surgical instruments, jokes, and various bric-à-brac. Suddenly, a dark and alluring woman appears beside him. Unable to resist, he follows her through sordid back streets to a house where he apparently meets an unpleasant end—probably surgical mutilation. The central portion of the story, set in the covered street, constitutes a separate, timeless world situated outside of the 14 July celebrations going on in the surrounding city. The silence and stillness of the place, its abandoned air, the dusty and old-fashioned items on sale, the unusual glaucous light filtering through the glass canopy over the street all create the impression of a world apart. The reader shares the narrator's feelings when he says: "I no longer had any notion of the time elapsed since I had entered the passage Pommeraye."

"Le Diamant," a story in *Feu de braise*, although a fairly brief tale, is complex in its symbolism and in its alchemical and mythical allusions. It tells of Sarah Mose, a diamond merchant's daughter, who has the same affinity with precious stones as Rebecca does with growing things. Her father always gives her his most valuable acquisitions to examine, and, one day, he asks her to look at a particularly magnificent diamond. After a ritual fast and cleansing, she strips off her clothes and goes into the room where the diamond is kept. As she is examining it, she seems to faint and fall forwards. When she recovers, she has shrunk in size and is now actually inside the diamond. She waits in the freezing cold as the sunlight entering the room slowly approaches the diamond. When it strikes the stone's surface, a tiny naked man appears, a man with a strangely leonine appearance. Telling her that she will be the mother of a child who will be the savior of her race, he couples with Sarah, holding her arms out as though she is being crucified. Then the sun passes on, the man disappears, and Sarah faints again. She recovers consciousness outside the diamond, which now has a tiny flaw in it. As the days pass, the flaw grows, as does the child inside her.

Easily recognizable in this story are the familiar themes of ritual, sacrifice, and relations with the natural world. Our point here, however, is to indicate the timeless nature of the incident inside the diamond. Sarah has left her watch in her bedroom and has no idea of how long she spends in the room. Once absorbed by the diamond, she can gauge time only roughly by the approach of the sunlight. The whole of the central incident is apart from the flow of time, and events take place with a dreamlike disregard for temporality.[2]

But Mandiargues does not stop at setting certain incidents outside of time, as in these two stories. Sometimes he seems to want to destroy the very idea of temporal duration. In *Mascarets*, one whole story, "Le Marronnier," consists of a discussion of time by three characters who wonder whether it is possible for people simply to disappear from time. This would have the effect of altering the past, and this consideration leads them to imagine people who had never existed suddenly appearing in the past. They then discuss whether man can change the flow of time (and, behind this, we recognize a typical surrealist preoccupation with the effect of man's will and imagination on the real world). These three characters have all removed their watches, and the discussion takes place at an indeterminate stage of the day, somewhere between the end of daylight and the beginning of nightfall. But the conversation makes it clear that the characters are interested in more than creating a timeless zone in their lives: they want nothing less than the destruction of temporal categories.

Certain other stories show Mandiargues trying to achieve this very goal in his fiction. The narrator of "Le Triangle ambigu," another work in *Mascarets*, meets a woman whom he finds very attractive, and he persuades her to come home with him. Just as she is about to leave with him, she realizes that she has seen him in a recurring dream in which she always kills him. Afraid the dream may come true, she now refuses his invitation. A dream experienced in the past thus intrudes into the present and destroys an anticipated future.[3] In *Soleil des loups* there is a story called "L'Etudiante" in which the heroine, Marie Mors, is able to see future events taking place in the window of a nearby house. She herself figures in these events, which invariably come true. Time, therefore, has little meaning for her, since she is able to live the future now. In one scene, she sees herself reading an album containing images of her and of the dreams she has had. In other words, she sees in the present a future in which she contemplates images of the past. She also sees a scene depicting her own disappearance from time, and this too comes to pass.

In some of Mandiargues's more fanciful tales, it is not even clear whether events have a place in time, whether they have really happened. "Les Formes charnelles" from *Mascarets* is the story of a man who seems to be watching a striptease show while his mind dwells on a murder that he has just committed. Or could it be that he is being questioned by the police about the murder, and that he is imagining the striptease scenes in order to evade the questions? In either case, we cannot be sure what is real and what is imagined. At the end of *Marbre*, a similar situation is created. The author suggests a possible ending for his novel, while indicating that the reader may invent another one if he wishes. The hero's future varies with the individual reader.

Most of the stories quoted so far contain an atmosphere of dream-like uncertainty. This contributes to the impression that they defy chronology, for, in dreams, time as we know it in the waking world has no place. Indeed, dreams may be seen as a manifestation of the unconscious, which, to use Thomas Mann's words, "knows no time, no temporal flow, nor any effect of time upon its psychic process."[4] Scenes such as the one in "Le passage Pommeraye" in which the narrator enters the mysterious street or the one in which Marie Mors disappears take place as though in a dream. All points of reference with the outside world, which might indicate the passage of time, are, as in a dream, removed from the narrative.

In addition to the generally blurred temporal framework of much of Mandiargues's fiction there are certain erotic scenes which stand out because they are particularly devoid of temporality. In *La Motocyclette*, when Daniel goes to bed with Rebecca, he first takes off his watch. When he meets her later in the Turkish bath, he is annoyed to discover that she is wearing a watch, and he makes her remove it, saying that "she had placed herself outside of the time of her usual life, and there could be no question of her keeping on her person an instrument that tied her to that time." In "Le Diamant," Sarah Mose removes her watch before she falls into the diamond. The heroine of *Le Lis de mer*, when she exposes her naked body to the man looking through the window, has also taken off her watch, and, when she goes to meet him, she leaves it behind because "it was not fitting to keep the free use of time and to keep the power to measure on a dial fixed to her wrist the hours and minutes swallowed up in sacrificial offering and servitude." The man in "La Marée" *(Mascarets)* removes his watch and sets it beside him when he and his cousin embark on their sexual escapade. To complete the list, one might mention "La Grotte," a tale in *Porte dévergondée* in which the hero, as he has sexual relations with a prostitute, is asked by her what time it is. He angrily replies that he does not wear a watch, and that "there is no time where we are."

These incidents all depict sexual activity as something which halts the progress of time. As Jean de Lugio in "Le Marronnier" puts it, sex is "the illusion of the continuity of the present." Lovers, Mandiargues says, seek to prolong the present moment and make its pleasure last forever. "One can agree," he writes in *Le Belvédère*, "that the art of lovers is, as they say, to 'make pleasure last,' but, in that case, it consists of a multitude of exquisite and splendid moments, without a past or a future." The writer who tries to capture truly erotic moments in his work must convey a present consisting of repeated moments of sexual ecstasy, and Mandiargues quotes Sade's work and Pierre Louÿs's *Trois filles de leur mère* as examples.

Mandiargues's attempts to manipulate time, to destroy temporal categories, and to halt chronology are all a response to the approach of death. The march of time has always obsessed and anguished mankind because it leads inevitably to death and the disappearance of the individual. A story like "L'Etudiante," behind its fantasy, is shot through with the awareness of passing time and approaching death. Marie Mors, as her name implies, is destined to die before the story ends, and her strange relationship with time makes her all the more aware that this is her fate. But, insofar as the erotic can halt time and plunge individuals into a continuous present, it is the supreme means of holding death at bay, almost an antidote to it.

Eroticism is also a response to death because it is an expression of the life forces. Mandiargues writes in one essay in *Troisième Belvédère* that: "love and sex are the first witnesses to life." He quotes Georges Bataille's words that eroticism is "the approval of life unto death," and he defines eroticism in another essay in the same volume as "the exaltation of the sexes through antagonism to death and in association with the life instinct." For him, woman's body, with its erotic connotations, is the very image of the will to live. Writing of primitive men, who depicted naked female forms on cave walls, he says: "It is quite marvelous that it should be precisely that image that man wanted (or needed) to impose on the rock, in that far-off time, when, as he became aware of death and invented the tomb, he realized that he was alive. The simple outline of a woman's body is the first affirmation of the awareness of life."

All these themes—sex as the affirmation of life, the destruction of temporal categories, the creation of a timeless present, the representation of lived time—are brought together in *La Marge*, Mandiargues's most ambitious novel and the one for which he was awarded the *Prix Goncourt*. This work tells how Sigismond Pons, replacing his sick cousin for a few days, goes to Barcelona on a business trip. While there, he receives a letter from his old governess. When he opens it, his eyes fall on a few lines that unmistakably indicate that his wife has killed herself. He immediately folds the letter and puts it in his pocket without reading any more. Now begins a period of several days spent wandering around Barcelona, especially in the prostitutes' quarter, where he uses the services of a certain Juanita, whom he picks up in a bar. He deliberately creates a timeless period set "in the margin" of his real life. This ends after three days when he opens the letter and reads that his son has accidentally drowned and his wife committed suicide. He gets in his car, drives to the outskirts of the city, and shoots himself.

It is hard to accept that a man, on hearing of a beloved wife's death, could blot out the knowledge so completely as Sigismond does. But it is not psychological depth that the author seeks in this novel. It is not a work of psychological realism any more than are his tales of people being absorbed by diamonds or seeing their future in a window. He weaves, instead, a novel of symbolic references which point beyond this kind of realism to the nature of life itself and man's experience of it.

Using again a technique reminiscent of the *nouveau roman*, Mandiargues shows us, in *La Marge*, one man's experience of time, sex, and death. He describes minutely the streets, people, bars, brothels, nightclubs, and restaurants of Barcelona, filling his pages with objects and concrete details as Robbe-Grillet or Butor do in their novels. We experience the city as Sigismond experiences it, and see things as they strike his consciousness. When the sights around him provoke memories of his honeymoon in Rome, his married life with Sergine, his childhood, and his relationship with a domineering and feared father, we relive these memories with him.

The core of *La Marge* is Sigismond's attempt to blot out awareness of his wife's death. He tries to shut himself up in a protective cover "as though he were in a transparent bubble." He uses sex as a weapon against death, for his wanderings around Barcelona are all centered on sexual activity: observation of the prostitutes, visits to bars and striptease shows, and use of the prostitute called Juanita. The Columbus monument, which dominates the novel as it does Barcelona, is used to convey the sexual message. It is a phallic presence looming over Sigismond's activities, and Mandiargues has described it in *Le Désordre de la mémoire* as "the most characteristically and colossally phallic monument that has ever been set up anywhere in the world." Even the Spanish word for Columbus, *Colón*, is pronounced much the same way, Mandiargues points out, as the French word for *column*. The very name of the famous discoverer thus has phallic connotations. It is significant, therefore, that the first thing that Sigismond does when he realizes that his wife is dead is make for this monument. In front of it, he sees a notice inviting visitors to take the elevator to the top, where Columbus's statue stands. Sigismond decides in *La Marge* that he "will accept the invitation all the more readily because he has just discovered an exorcising force in the name of Colón, and because it seems beneficent to get close to the statue, especially by the highly virile method proposed by the notice." After his visit, he buys a bottle of liqueur shaped like the Columbus monument, and, on returning to his hotel, he takes out his letter and places the bottle on top of it. The phallic bottle seals the letter holding tidings of death, and only when he removes it to read the letter does Sigismond accept that his own death must be its necessary consequence.

In this novel, and in all of Mandiargues's fiction, sex represents the life forces *within* man. But it is also an antidote to death because erotic activity puts individuals in contact with the life forces *outside* of man. The curious little tale "Le Pont" in *Le Musée noir* illustrates this point quite aptly. Its hero, Damien, once lived in the city, an artificial and sterile life far from the "panic" forces inherent in the natural world. One day, he went to a bar where it was the custom for men to challenge women employees to a game of billiards. If a man won (which rarely happened), he was allowed to sleep with the woman. On this occasion, the woman took a fancy to Damien and let him win. He discovered, however, that he was impotent.

Now Damien lives in the country, where he spends much of his time brooding in the woods near an apparently abandoned bridge. His meditation is interrupted when a beautiful woman rides by on a horse. Fascinated, he follows her to an old castle. He learns that she is called Camille de Hur, and, as the days pass, he is drawn more and more to her castle. The forest now seems to come alive with erotic forces; he sees a tree whose forked trunk reminds him of open legs and whose roots look like Camille's hair. He discovers three bird's eggs in a nest, and achieves an intensely erotic pleasure by breaking one of them over the forked trunk. He then makes his way to Camille's castle bearing a bouquet of flowers with the two remaining eggs in it. (These eggs are fertility symbols representing a life and vigor missing when he lived in the city.) He gains entrance by an open window and is greeted by Camille. That night he sleeps with her and discovers that he is no longer impotent. He finds union with the life-giving "panic" forces incarnated by the woman, who is described in "Le Pont" as part of the natural world, "more precious than all the other creatures of the forest."

Loss of communion with these forces can, on the other hand, produce death. The next morning, Damien meets Camille's husband, a cruel, cold man whose sole delight is to hunt the forest animals. He incarnates anti-"panic" powers, all that would come between man and life. He makes Damien accompany him into the forest, where he has his servants destroy the bridge that represents Damien's link to Camille and the forces of nature. Damien turns dejectedly towards home, his new-found strength ebbing, while the other man seems to grow younger and more vigorous. He suddenly begins to cough and spit blood, and we realize that he is now doomed to die because his access to the "panic" forces has been destroyed.

"Les Pierreuses," a very brief story in *Feu de braise*, makes the same point. Pascal Bénin is walking in the countryside one freezing cold day when he hears a cry coming from a stone lying beside the path. He picks it up, takes it home, and cracks it open. Out spring three tiny, naked female figures whose perfect forms fill him with a flush of sexual excitement. They address him in Latin, explaining that they have issued naked from their mother and that Pascal must die because he has released them from the stone. Pascal immediately assumes that their mother is nature itself and that they are manifestations of its power. Suddenly, they are consumed by flames, and Pascal throws himself on his bed, knowing he must die. His death is a result of his inability to commune (either in language or sexually) with these creatures who are the forces of nature.[5]

The erotic is a barrier to death, but it is also indissolubly linked to it as well. In an important article in *Le Cadran lunaire* called "Eros noir" Mandiargues discusses Bataille's conception of the erotic, and approves his contention that eroticism is closely tied to death. There is, Mandiargues argues, a type of eroticism, which he calls "black eros," that has a dark, tragic side because it carries with it the promise of death. This is, he says, "the point of view which seems to me the only one from which the question can be accurately considered."

Because it leads to loss of the sense of personal identity, a kind of momentary oblivion that foreshadows the final snuffing out of life, the sex act bears similarities to death. Sex and death have always been linked in man's mind, and, in French, one expression for orgasm is *la petite mort*. Mandiargues knows very well that he is not espousing an original point of view, but he sees this association as a powerful inspiration to the artist. He says in *Le Désordre de la mémoire*: "Much more than a theme, it is rather a notion buried in the darkest unconscious and it is one of the most generous sources of inspiration to which poets, narrators, and artists can have recourse." Not surprisingly, in his own work death is as constant a presence as eroticism. It is always there, in the background, casting its shadow over every couple, over every sexual act and erotic allusion.

Often the close link between these two is established by brief references, images, and comparisons. In *La Marge*, for example, Sigismond compares women's sexual organs to "an open tomb"; the hotel where the man in "La Grotte" takes the prostitute is called Sarcophage Hotel; in *La Motocyclette* Rebecca describes a car she passes as a "coffin bed"; when she sees the spilled blood of her virginity on the bed sheet, she thinks of it as being "as black as on a several-hundred-year-old shroud."

Certain stories are based mainly on the premise that sexual experience and death are identical. In "Armoire de lune," a story in *Mascarets*, a couple make love on a tomb, which opens and swallows them. In "Le Nu parmi les cercueils" from *Feu de braise* a man has a vision of a voluptuous naked woman surrounded by coffins. She tells him that she is kept prisoner by an undertaker, who forces her to perform striptease acts among the coffins before he has his pleasure with her. The girl points out that undertakers' premises are frequently situated in the prostitutes' quarter because "it is well known that nothing inspires man with the desire for prostitutes as much as imagining his death, or that of his acquaintances." As Jean de Juni in "L'Enfantillage," another tale from *Feu de braise*, has intercourse with a prostitute, his mind turns to scenes of death that he has witnessed in his childhood: a pet tortoise run over by a truck, a pig being slaughtered, an ox cart fallen into a ravine. In *Mascarets*, "La Révélation" tells of a woman painter who does portraits of all her lovers in a paint which turns black. When she dies, she intends to have them buried with her, and certain herbs in the coffin will restore the pictures. Her body will corrupt, surrounded by portraits of her lovers, and when her bones pierce the skin, any lovers still left alive will die.

But it is Mandiargues's first novel, *Marbre*, which demonstrates most completely the identity of life, sex, and death. *Marbre* is a rambling work consisting of several separate episodes linked only by the central character. This technique is often associated with the picaresque novel, and, indeed, the hero is in many ways a modern picaro. He wanders around the country (in this case, Italy), finding sexual adventure, mocking society's accepted code of conduct, taking advantage of women. His attitude toward women is one of cynical exploitation, and his keenest delight is to inflame his fiancée's desires, only to leave her abruptly when she makes sexual advances. With other women, he does not hesitate to respond to the desire he provokes, and, because of these sexual proclivities, Mandiargues compares him to a goat. His very name underscores the comparison. He is called Ferréol Buq, a name that suggests *bouc*— French for a goat. However, like the picaro, Ferréol learns certain lessons about life, and the most important of these is that life and death, sex and death are bound together, and that they are all incarnated by woman.

The first hints of this lesson come in a series of dreams. In one, he finds a huge skull, which bursts into flower and this makes him think: "The god Pan is about to be reborn." In another dream, he enters a room where he expects to find a Chinese prostitute, but, when he pulls aside the curtain hiding her bed, he discovers a goat's skull.[6] The lesson begins in earnest when he is driving in an isolated part of southern Italy and a wizened old man stops him. He shows Ferréol an invitation to witness the death of Dona Lavinia D'Alba, an invitation gruesomely ornamented with a baroque profusion of skeletons and superimposed with a sun resembling a skull. Ferréol agrees to take the old man to the hill town where the ceremony is to take place.

On the way, they pass menhirs painted with skeletons holding the hands of pregnant women, symbolizing the interconnection of fecundity and death. Ferréol senses that he is approaching some mysterious revelation, and "for a moment, the space of a swift's flight, he felt he was about to discover some deep and tragic truth." He glimpses that the meaning of these strange monuments and of his earlier dreams will soon become clear, and that it is not unconnected with the role that women have played in his life. Then they encounter another monument: a huge egg on which are sculpted crucified pregnant women. When they reach the town, Ferréol notices a fountain shaped like a skull from which flows a stream of water. Then he is taken to an arena where the dying Dona Lavinia is brought to breathe her last before an audience consisting only of men.

Once again we recognize the familiar ritual setting: an arena which was once a church but which now "houses mysteries that have no relationship with the official religion," a raised platform in the middle of the arena, and men seated in tiers all around it. Dona Lavinia's husband enters dressed in an antique uniform and followed by his son and two nephews bearing the dying woman. Behind them is the doctor. Dona Lavinia is placed on the platform, and, in tense silence, the assembly watches her death throes. The atmosphere is electric with sexual excitement, and Ferréol himself is "seized completely by the exaltation and the delirium of the people around him." The woman's body is shaken by spasms resembling sexual ecstacy, and the men are "all gasping." After the final spasm, the men avoid looking at each other, and there can be sensed a "curious release of tension which reminded Ferréol of certain states he had himself passed through, but in circumstances far removed from a woman's death."

Ferréol had previously compared the arena to a bullring, and had commented that the moment of the kill in a bullfight is known as "the moment of truth." Dona Lavinia's death is precisely one such moment for him. After his earlier callous attitude toward women, he has now seen the "black" side of eroticism. Mandiargues deliberately constructs a ritual, semireligious scene of the type he usually reserves for erotic incidents and uses it to depict a woman's death. The lesson he teaches Ferréol is that life, sex, and death are inseparable, and this mystery is revealed in the marvelous, almost sacred body of woman.

But if eroticism is linked to death, what of the forces which pour into Mandiargues's characters during moments of sexual ecstasy? We have already seen that separation from them can result in death. Other stories indicate that contact with them can also be deadly, for, like erotic experience itself, these forces contain within them the power of death. They are potentially dangerous, and to offend them is to invite punishment. Hence, when Marceline's parents transgress against them by killing the rabbit through which she maintains "panic" communion, they have to die. The Negro too dies because he has unleashed forces beyond his ken and because these forces no longer need him. Marceline, on the other hand, is protected by her very innocence.

The same pattern of offense and punishment may be seen in "L'Opéra des falaises" from *Soleil des loups*. Captain Idalium has led a life of callous cruelty towards women, and has committed a variety of vicious acts towards the animal kingdom. The "panic" forces, which often choose animals or women as their instruments, are offended by this behavior. That he is inimical to them is seen by the fact that, when he approaches a compass, it always veers from its normal course. He, in turn, fears these forces, especially when they show themselves in storms. One day, he follows a beautiful woman in the expectation of sexual adventure, and she leads him to a cave, where he is set upon and imprisoned by some animals. In a setting of ritualistic horror, in the midst of a rocky arena, the animals act out scenes representing his crimes, then kill him. It is in this way that the powers he has wronged strike back at him.

In *Marbre*, Ferréol Buq has offended the same forces by his treatment of women, and his realization of the marvelous mystery they represent may have come too late. Although the reader is invited to invent his own ending to *Marbre*, Mandiargues suggests one possibility that we may see as a form of punishment. He proposes that Ferréol meet a beautiful woman too, and that he follow her to a spot which was once an arena or a place of religious sacrifice. Here Ferréol might meet his death in "a kind of natural orgasm (earthquake, a volcanic phenomenon common in this area, storm, or huge wave from the sea)." Such catastrophes are manifestations of the telluric powers that Ferréol has aroused by his attitude to women.

To sum up the points covered in this chapter we must return to Rebecca Nul and *La Motocyclette*, in which Mandiargues gives his most moving representation of the identity of life, sex, and death through the "panic" forces. The final goal of Rebecca's journey, the cataclysmic event to which her quest, unknown to her, is leading, is not a meeting with Daniel, but her own death. The novel ends when she skids into the back of a truck and is killed. But, in this moment, she receives a blinding, split second of revelation that enables her to see the true nature of life and of the "panic" forces in the world.

On the back of the truck that kills Rebecca is painted a face of Bacchus, the trademark of the beer that it is carrying. This grinning face seems to swallow her when she hurtles into it, and, as she dies, she suddenly thinks: "The universe is Dionysiac." The face appears to her as "a human, or a superhuman face, the last, perhaps the true face of the universe." Now Bacchus is Dionysus under a different name, and both may be identified with Pan. All three represent the forces of creation, the divine power flowing into the world.[7] At her moment of death, Rebecca encounters those very life forces that she has met in her moments of sexual union with Daniel. As if to underline that these are the same, Mandiargues describes Rebecca's death agony (like Dona Lavinia's) as though it were an erotic experience. We are told that, "thousands of blades plunge into her and it seems that they make one single wound through which her lover spreads into her."

Rebecca's realization that the world is Dionysiac represents acceptance that the forces of life are also the forces of death. Life, death, and sex are linked in this story, as they are throughout Mandiargues's fiction, because they are all manifestations of the same powers in the universe.

References to Dionysus, Pan, and Bacchus also draw the reader's attention to another level of the novel which reinforces the message contained in Rebecca's death. One of the many possible interpretations of this multifaceted novel is that it recounts a mythical journey to the underworld. Dionysus, in ancient myth, was killed and dismembered by Titans, but was resurrected by Zeus. He represents, therefore, life in death. Like many figures of myth (Orpheus, Isis, Persephone, and Christ), he journeyed into death and returned to life. Rebecca's journey retraces this mythical one. She thinks of the river that she crosses as being like the "infernal river which must be crossed by the soul after death according to most religions." The frontier she passes may be seen as the entrance to Hell, for the customs official is depicted as a cold, frightening guardian. On his finger he wears a ring bearing a serpent (a creature sacred to Isis), and Rebecca immediately realizes that it is "placed under the sign of death." Most mythical heroes who visit the underworld finally return, and their journey contains the promise of life in death. In Rebecca's case, her realization that life and death are one can be seen as this promise.

Mandiargues is acutely aware of death. Indeed, he says that whenever he begins a novel, he knows that it may never be finished, since death could always intervene. It is for this reason that he writes in *Troisième Belvédère*: "Consciousness of the novel seems to me inseparable from consciousness of death." But, although death is one of the constants of his fiction, a familiar of all his characters, and the basis of his own awareness of life, and although he often manipulates time and uses sexual activity in his fiction as a barrier against death, it is not feared by him. He sees it in *Le Désordre de la mémoire* as a natural part of life, as "the greatest marvel one can expect from life." It is an ever present part of his fiction because, as he puts it in *Deuxième Belvédère,* it is "the virtual and yet essential companion of man." Unlike many modern writers (Malraux, Camus, Céline, and others), who see death as the ultimate proof of the absurdity of existence, Mandiargues accepts it quite naturally as part of man's life. He refuses to treat it with horror or anguish, but says: "It seems to me that death is a very ordinary happening in the face of which it is not necessary to assume an air to fit the circumstances."[8] He has praised Supervielle in *Deuxième Belvédère* because he treats death as "a close relative," but the same could be said of Mandiargues himself. This attitude produces a certain serenity, a calmness in the presence of death which is unusual in modern fiction, but which makes Mandiargues's work refreshingly different.

Mandiargues touches on some of the most fundamental issues in his fiction, showing us his conception of the very nature of life, of the forces governing it, and of man's relationship to these forces. His is a difficult and apparently contradictory view of existence that sees life and death as one, but he succeeds admirably in conveying it. In so doing, he shows that "serious" literature need not be one of abstruse arguments, philosophical digressions, or metaphysical ramblings. A whole attitude toward life and a deeply felt intuition about the forces surrounding us are expressed with brio, humor, and an inimitable sense of the fantastic.

4

Escape from the Self

The urge to transcend self-conscious self-hood is . . . a principal appetite
of the soul.   Aldous Huxley, *The Doors of Perception*

IT HAS PROBABLY OCCURRED to the reader by this point that much of
Mandiargues's fiction is an attempt to escape the limits of the self.
When his characters open themselves to the "panic" powers and commune with the natural world, they are breaking out of the bounds im-
posed on them by their individual identity. They are no longer isolated
individuals, but part of a greater, more all-embracing reality. Likewise,
when they create for themselves a world set apart from the flow of time,
or when they destroy the categories of time altogether, they are releasing
themselves from one of the most inhibiting factors in human existence.
He who escapes the tyranny of time has certainly succeeded in transcending his essence as an individual, for the individual is continually
swept along by the hours and the days, hampered in his freedom of
movement by the pressure of the seconds, his ability to do what he will
curtailed by his imprisonment in temporal flow.

One frequent occurrence in Mandiargues's fiction, a very basic
technique of his fantasy, is a sudden change of shape by his characters.
This too is connected with the theme of escape from individual identity.
When Sarah Mose shrinks and is absorbed by a precious stone; when the
narrator of "Le Pain rouge", a story in *Soleil des loups,* is stung by an
insect and becomes tiny enough to enter a crust of bread; when Ferréol
Buq, in one of his dreams, is changed into wood; when the man in
"L'Homme du parc Monceau" from *Le Musée noir* assumes any shape at
will, they are all realizing a desire to break the bonds of their unique
individuality.

Mandiargues's is an art of the fantastic, where anything may happen. Fantasy and fantastic art may themselves be seen as a manifestation
of the desire to escape all the inhibiting rules of existence, for they are
obviously based on the premise that the "impossible" may happen.
Among these inhibiting rules is the one that an individual is who he is,

39

and nothing more. The longing to lose this sense of self rings through Mandiargues's fiction, and may be heard like a plaintive cry in many of his tales of fantasy. The heroine of *La Motocyclette*, for example, is reduced by the sheer speed of her motorcycle to a blessed sense of nonbeing, until she becomes "a poor child thrown like a stone into emptiness." Vanina, as she lies naked before her future lover in *Le Lis de mer*, is so motionless that "it seemed to her that she had left her body." Sarah Mose in "Le Diamant" *(Feu de braise)* also achieves a stillness so intense that "she lost all notion of time and forgot to listen to her heart." In such states, all points of reference in time and space disappear. Hence, Titus Perle in "L'hypnotiseur," a story in *Sous la lame*, walked about in a trance in which "he lost all notion of the geographic point where he was," while Jean de Lugio in "Le Marronnier" *(Mascarets)* longs to be "annihilated in the past at the same time as in the present, and thus never to have had the least atom of an existence which one curses all day long."

Eroticism must obviously have a privileged place in this attempt to escape the confines of self, as it does in Mandiargues's work as a whole. He sees it as a way of reaching out beyond the self to another level of being where individual identity no longer exists. He says in *Le Cadran lunaire* that "the tremendous appeal of eroticism (of that black eros) is that it finally leads to loss of the personality." Erotic experience, he goes on, "makes you slip, to your delight, through the narrow opening, into another world where *you are no longer yourself*" (italics in original). In his own works, there are many examples of this process. One might quote, for instance, the scene witnessed by the narrator of "Le Pain rouge" *(Soleil des loups)*: several men, with bees swarming all over them, are experiencing an erotic pleasure so intense that they are no longer in control of themselves, and they display "such an exquisite enjoyment that the expression of it could only be compared to a saint's when she is seen in the midst of the most convulsive ecstasy." Sometimes the erotic is mingled with a sense of peace and blessed stillness produced by escape from one's usual limits. One character in "La Grotte" *(Porte dévergondée)* achieves, in the act of sex, "a kind of nothingness or emptiness," while Jean de Juni, the hero of "L'Enfantillage" *(Feu de braise)*, uses a prostitute to reach a state in which "his spirit tended towards a kind of zero, as though for a sort of mystic union with the nullity of his partner." In "Adive" from *Mascarets*, a woman at the height of sexual pleasure (provoked, in this case, by a dog) feels both emptiness and beatitude: "Stéphanie descends into emptiness and comes up again, until she is engulfed and exalted by a feeling of beatitude which is both a bottommost point and a summit."

As we have seen, the erotic for Mandiargues nearly always has connotations of death, and this too represents the final loss of self. When

Rebecca crashes into the truck, when Sigismond shoots himself, and when Ferréol Buq dies in an earthquake, they achieve the escape from their own being that they have already glimpsed in their moments of erotic pleasure. It is in these supreme, culminating points of their lives that they become one with the world, that they cease to be separate entities cut off from the forces of the universe. They illustrate Bataille's idea that "dying and breaking out of one's limits are, moreover, the same thing."[1] In his own life, Mandiargues has felt the temptation of death as the ultimate escape from the self. In *Le Désordre de la mémoire* he tells how, as a young man, he would lie on the cliff top at Berneval, hanging out over the emptiness beneath him, imagining his body falling into the void.[2]

For Mandiargues, there is nothing unnatural in this urge to break the bonds of one's identity. Indeed, he sees it as a fundamental instinct, expressed eloquently by the character in "L'Homme du parc Monceau," when he is seized by "that old pagan sadness, which often wrings a groan from those whose destiny is to be unique in the face of all other species in the world." In a commentary to a book on Léonor Fini's masks, he examines this instinct with great depth of feeling, arguing that all men are smitten, at times, by ontological anguish which makes them long, with their whole being, to throw off the individual traits, the personality, and the body that are theirs. He writes with real Baudelairian spleen:

> There are hours in our life . . . when there can be felt the imperious need to break out of our selves, when we are finally ashamed of the personality in which birth has deposited us and habit imprisoned us, of the species to which we belong (are there so many reasons, by the way, for being proud of this? This word *belong* that stinks of vulgarity a mile away. . . . This word *imprisoned* that reeks of the galley-slave. . . . What odors it all gives off!), moments when we are assailed by the tedium of a sexual identity that is always despairingly the same, of the unchanging drama and the comedy that it has got us into since our adolescence. There are hours when we bring our face close to the mirror until the cold glass sends a shiver through our skin, and we are weary, absolutely weary, of the image that we see in the silvering of the mirror, of the monotonous features that it has always reflected, except that they are a little more faded every year, of that forehead behind whose bones floats a curtain of old ideas that we would like to destroy, of those eyes, of that look, of that mouth from which all the words that could flow are already known.[3]

Mandiargues points out that men have traditionally sought to satisfy this deep-seated urge to break the bonds of selfhood in two ways:

by playing games and by wearing masks. Both these activities enable the individual to become someone else, to assume momentarily another identity. Mandiargues quotes the example of Léonor Fini, who, when she wears one of her masks, seems actually to become the animal represented by the mask. At such moments, "both her gestures and her look show eloquently the happiness that she feels at no longer seeming herself, at finding herself *at last* in another's skin."[4] In *Deuxième Belvédère* he writes that masks represent an attempt on the part of man "to break with himself and to change into something else, to escape from himself, or at least from the space, environment and laws which are normally part of him." Even the underwater swimmer's face mask plays this role, for it enables him to enter a world where "he discovers a perspective, dimensions, light which are absolutely new to him."[5]

Another traditional means of escaping the bonds of self, and one that particularly appeals to Mandiargues, is the use of drugs. The fact that, in certain societies, drugs have always been used shows that "men were no sooner dressed in their bodies than they felt the need to escape from them" (*Le Cadran lunaire*). Drugs, masks, and certain kinds of mental disturbance all, paradoxically, reveal the true nature of man; they all show that in the heart of every individual is a wish to be other than he is. In *Troisième Belvédère* he writes: "Various mental disturbances, . . . the delirium, and aberrations produced artificially by drugs are also masks which, by setting man outside of himself, by stripping him of the covering he shares with others, reveal his deepest being."

Although such terms as "religious" and "mystic" are not ones that one would normally associate with Mandiargues, and although in *Le Désordre de la mémoire* he has denied being a "man of faith," the longing that he describes so movingly in his essays and captures in all its heart-rending intensity in his fiction bears a marked resemblance to the mystic's search for a way to go beyond this life and the limits it imposes on him. Indeed, even the erotic obsession in his work can be seen, not as something that sets him apart from such writers, but as a common bond with them. It has frequently been pointed out that religious and sexual ecstasy are almost indistinguishable, and that there are obvious erotic overtones in the moment of union with the godhead recounted by the great Spanish mystics. Bataille, while denying that such union is nothing but sublimated sexuality, agrees that there are "flagrant similarities, even equivalences and links, between the systems of erotic and mystic outpouring."[6] He also points out that the goal of both religion and the orgies of primitive societies is to produce a loss of the sense of self in the participants.[7] In light of this, one may see the whole of *L'Anglais décrit dans le château fermé*, which is a series of repeated sexual orgies, as having a kind of religious basis. In *Le Belvédère* Mandiargues describes another such work, by a different writer, as being mystic. He argues that, in Pauline Réage's *Histoire d'O*, the heroine's willingness to be stripped of her individual humanity and to become a mere object shows a definite semireligious longing to become the zero which her very name suggests.

Mandiargues is neither unacquainted with nor unattracted by certain aspects of mystic experience. Much of the art that he appreciates has a mystico-religious side that he is at pains to point out. In *Troisième Belvédère* he praises the work of the Mexican artist Toledo as "a mystic endeavor, which is of the same order as the profoundest clairvoyant vision." Three other artists whom he especially singles out for praise are Tapies, Milares, and Burri, who have, he says in *Deuxième Belvédère,* "a spiritual vision as intense as that of poets or mystics." Dada, a movement which, as a precursor of the surrealists, has always exercised a special interest for him, is described as: "The last mystic current to which the Western world has been able to give birth and which made its impetus felt there before being engulfed." As for the surrealists themselves, many of whose ideas and intuitions he shares, he praises them in *Le Belvédère* for saying that modern man must "pay attention to the voices that preserve an echo of ancient revelations . . . turn toward the teaching of the occultists, the alchemists, and of certain mystics and illuminati."

Mandiargues is not a "religious" writer in the conventional sense. He does not advocate a specific religion or profess belief in a god. He does believe, however, that there are in the universe powers that are greater than man, mysterious forces that men can sometimes sense, and he says in *Deuxième Belvédère* that "the human spirit is naturally inclined towards the supernatural." He gives credence to such ancient beliefs as astrology precisely because it shows an awareness of these powers.[8] These are the forces that may be seen in the "panic" incidents described in his fiction. Indeed, it is almost as though Mandiargues becomes their tool when he writes about them. He appears to be describing more than the inspiration that all artists feel when he says in *Troisième Belvédère* that, when he is writing, "I know that I am gripped, every time, by something stronger than myself."

Care must, nevertheless, be taken not to overemphasize this "religious" side of his vision.[9] Christian mystics seek to escape both themselves and a life in which they are held prisoner; they seek union with a transcendent deity who exists beyond this world and this life. Mandiargues's characters do not look for that kind of escape. What interests them is release from their individual identities so that they may become a part of the world. They look for communion with forces inherent in creation, not with a force transcending it. What grips them is a furious desire, an almost sexual avidity for the surrounding universe. When Vanina and Rebecca give themselves to their lovers, the ecstasy which seizes them is an expression of their passion for the world itself. Rebecca's death is described as an erotic, Dionysiac ecstasy, for this is her final possession by the forces within creation. It is fittingly described this way, for the ancient adherents of Dionysus celebrated in wild, frenzied worship their possession by the god who incarnated the forces of the world. During these moments in Mandiargues's fiction, the frontier between personal being and the life inherent in all things suddenly disappears. This experience, Mandiargues believes, is known by any sensitive artist, but especially by the painter. For him, the painter above all others tries to embrace the universe, to possess it, and become part of it; and in *Deuxième Belvédère* he sees Bona's early attempts to paint as "a sign of violent avidity, a mark of love as much as curiosity for the outside world."

This view of man, separate from the world but longing to be part of it, is merely one element in a broader view that represents life as a series of opposites. Mandiargues has a dualistic idea of creation, seeing things in terms of black and white, male and female, life and death, while believing that these pairs are part of a whole, dependent on each other and inseparable. His characters and the world from which they are separated, yet with which they achieve union, are simply one pair in this dualistic conception of being.

Once again, it is the artist who, in Mandiargues's opinion, has been instinctively aware of the dual nature of existence, for he often reflects it in his own character. In *Troisième Belvédère* Mandiargues talks of "that singular duality that has always in our opinion been the mark of superior minds and that is present anyway in the works that we have loved or that we love the most." Certain ancient religions and Christian heresies have also seen this duality, and Mandiargues writes with approval of "the belief in dualism or an antagonism inherent in the divinity, a divinity which, in the image of the double appearance of the planet Venus (Vesper or Lucifer), is divided between a force of light and a force of darkness, a power of good and a power of evil." In many religions, Mandiargues points out in *Deuxième Belvédère*, the dualism is symbolized by Venus: "The evening and the morning star, Venus was in the mythology of the ancient peoples of the Mediterranean the symbol of the duality, of the essential ambiguity of the universe, of the deep contrast one may see in nature."

Mandiargues feels the ambiguity of the universe so deeply that he believes that he shares it himself, and he is particularly attracted to Manichaean interpretations of existence, since they seem to explain this division. He says: "I feel everything in terms of opposites. It could be said that I have a Manichaeistic personality. Manichaeism is an old gnostic sect and is based on a play or tension of opposites. I see white and black together; heights and depths. When I look at myself in the mirror, I see that both sides of my face are different. I believe in the simultaneity of contraries."[10] In another interview he has expressed in similar terms his assessment of his own character: "I have, by the way, a rather double nature. You have not noticed, of course, but in photographs of me, there is half of my face that does not look like me at all. I have sometimes thought that I have half of my face in Hell and the other in some kind of Heaven."[11]

Many of Mandiargues's characters are, in this respect, created in his own image. Abel Foligno in "Mil neuf cent trente-trois", one of the stories in Sous la lame, is torn between love of his wife and the cruel urge to hurt her, and his sign is the evening star, "Venus . . . which is Hesperus or Vesper in the evening, Lucifer or Phosphorus before dawn . . . symbolic of the essential duality of good and evil." Sigismond Pons, hovering between life and death, divided by memories of his wife and of his father, possessed by both homosexual and heterosexual tendencies, is another such character. Marceline Caïn, the cold, innocent virgin who unleashes terrible forces and kills her own parents is yet another. Often the setting of the work reflects the same ambiguity, for Mandiargues has a definite predilection for times and places that are neither here nor there, that are indefinite, ill-defined, and balanced between two worlds. In Marbre Ferréol Buq spends several weeks on the seashore, in that area between high tide and low tide, that no-man's-land which is sometimes land and sometimes sea, "an intermediate place between one world and another, and which belonged to both of them." "La Marée" (Mascarets) is set in a similar area, transposed from space to time. The climax of the story takes place at high tide, precisely that moment which is neither before nor after, which is balanced on a knife-edge between the two movements of the tides. "Le Marronnier" is set at twilight, when it is neither day nor night, but when time partakes of both. Even one of Mandiargues's plays, La Nuit séculaire, takes place at another such time: during the night of 31 December 1899 when one century blends into another.

Perhaps the most fundamental polarity of human experience, the one that governs our awareness of life and is behind nearly all our psychic activity, is the division between male and female. Mandiargues sees this division within the world itself, and he refers, in order to express it, to ancient beliefs that associated the air (or sky) with light and with the masculine principle, and the waters with night and the feminine principle.[12] Certain artists, with their sensitivity to the forces in the world, have captured in their work the male/female duality. Mandiargues singles out as examples of such artists the Fontainebleau School, Bat-Yosef, and Miró.[13]

Several of the characters in his fiction bear this sexual duality within them, and are described almost as androgynous. For example, in *La Motocyclette* Rebecca has a distinctly masculine air, especially when she is dressed in motorcyclists' clothes that can be worn equally by a man. Her lover thinks of her as having "the traits of an Amazon," and her beauty is described as being "masculine" *(garçonnière)*. In *Le Désordre de la mémoire* Mandiargues himself refers to a "certain hermaphroditism" in his heroine. Sigismond, on the other hand, has a rather feminine appearance. Mandiargues writes that he is basically a "lunar" character, and that he has a strongly feminine side. His hermaphroditism is symbolized by the two people whose memory accompanies him: his wife and his father. Since his father was also a homosexual, they also represent the two tendencies within him: the homosexual and the heterosexual. Stéphanie, the main character in "Adive," also combines these two tendencies, since she has a male lover, yet she is attracted sexually to a girl she meets in the street. She first becomes aware of the girl as she is looking at a ring in a jeweler's window. The ring contains a moonstone surrounded by pearls that make it look like a sun. It thus has within it the masculine (sun) and feminine (moon) principles, and Stéphanie realizes that "the secret symbolism of the ring is certainly that of the hermaphrodite." In rather more startling fashion, the prostitute whose services Abel Foligno uses is also a hermaphrodite, since she wears a huge artificial phallus. Even the old man who leads Ferréol Buq to the hill town is ambiguous sexually, for he is beardless, has what appears to be breasts, and is referred to at one point as "she."

This dualistic view of life, expressed in terms of sexual divisions, throws further light on the erotic in Mandiargues's fiction. The sexual union that lies at the center of so much of his work may be seen as symbolic of the union of opposites in creation. The sex act is the very image of the unity behind the duality of nature as Mandiargues sees it. As we noted in chapter 1, eroticism for him is "the infinite community where good joins evil and where all things are rigorously the same." Clearly, the erotic in Mandiargues's work is a complex, multidimensional theme which may be interpreted in many different yet related ways.

We know that, always accompanying the erotic theme, is the one of death. Part of Mandiargues's dualistic interpretation of existence is the idea that life and death are one. This idea has already been examined in some depth, so there is no need to go over it again, except to point it out as further evidence of the dualism that he sees in life. Reference must be made, however, to a symbolic representation of the life/death duality that occurs in several tales. This symbol is the egg, which plays a particularly important role in *La Marge* and *Marbre*. Mandiargues, talking of *La Marge*, says: "Everything in the novel alludes to the egg which, as you know, symbolizes both life and death. Life is nurtured within the egg. It is protected by the shell, which preserves the embryo. If the egg is broken before the time is ripe, the life enclosed within it perishes.[14] The "bubble" with which Sigismond surrounds himself may be compared to the egg, for it keeps him alive until it is broken and death enters his life. When he visits the prostitute, he rolls an egg over her naked body, and this peculiar erotic game emphasizes the connection between the egg and the sexual forces representing life. In the museum at Barcelona, he sees a picture of the stoning of Saint Etienne, where the stones resemble eggs. Here they are clearly symbols of death. In *Marbre*, the egg-shaped monument stands for fertility and life, while the crucified pregnant women sculpted on it represent life and death. In one of his dreams, Ferréol breaks open an egg which splatters yolk all over him and gives off "a smell of death."

Death, in Mandiargues's scheme of things, is the final union of all opposites, the ultimate reconciliation of the apparent contradictions of life. When Rebecca dies, life and death, sexual ecstasy and the forces of destruction, she and Daniel, the male and the female are all united in one Dionysiac frenzy. Sigismond, in his death, achieves the reconciliation of all the contradictions of his life. The images of his father and his wife accompany him on his last journey to the place where he kills himself, and these two forces, which, until then, had seemed to war within him, now join together to urge him to his death. "A strange pair is constituted by these two," Mandiargues writes in *La Marge*, "a contradictory yet harmonized pair—whose current conjunction condemns Sigismond most inexorably."

As a final illustration of how Mandiargues's dualistic vision underlies his fiction, we might turn to "Le Diamant," that complex little tale on which we have already briefly touched. Among its many possible levels of meaning, it can be seen as an allegory of the alchemists' attempt to find the primeval matter behind all created things. We need not dwell on all the allusions to alchemy in the story, since they have already been covered more than adequately in an excellent article by Susan Campanini.[15] One or two points should be made, however. The uniting of opposites, which was the goal of alchemy, is seen in this tale when the sexual union of Sarah and the lion man takes place. The two characters are diametric opposites: Sarah is a cold, pure virgin, while the man is a warm figure born of the sun's rays. Sarah's ritual cleansing before she examines the diamond is akin to the alchemists' attempt to purify matter to the point where the primeval substance may be distilled. Her absorption by the diamond unites human and mineral—two apparently separate forms of created matter. It is fitting that this union should take place inside the diamond, for it can be seen as representing the Philosophers' Stone, the mystical substance that combines everything. The whole story is an excellent example of Mandiargues's erudition, his interest in occult knowledge, and hs effortless skill at weaving references to such knowledge into his fiction.[16]

"Le Diamant" is typical of Mandiargues's work as a whole, which is, in one of its most fundamental aspects, an attempt to reconcile all that is disparate. Like alchemy itself, it tries to take the duality, the pairs of apparent opposites that underlie existence, and synthesize them. His comment in *Troisième Belvédère* on the painter Le Maréchal, that he is "a Janus or a two-sided mirror where the least reconcilable of extremes meet with ease" is an equally valid comment on himself and his own work. And, here again, we may see an affinity with the surrealists, who tried to show the surprising, unseen relationships between apparently different elements of the world. To quote one critic: "One of the basic characteristics of the surrealist mind is its uncompromising will to find a foolproof unity in the universe."[17] She might be speaking of Mandiargues.

We seem to have come a long way from Mandiargues's "mystic" yearnings to the duality of existence, alchemy and the uniting of all the opposites of creation. Yet this journey is not as far and unlikely as it might at first appear. Everything is linked and bound by subtle ties in Mandiargues's work. The longing to escape the imprisonment of the self is part of the desire to reconcile opposites. When Rebecca, Vanina, and Sarah break out of their restricting envelope of personal identity and achieve "panic" communion with the world around them, they are participating in the union of opposites, in overcoming one of the most agonizing of dualities that plague man's existence: his alienation in a nonhuman world. They become part of that world, and, by so doing, they show the basic unity of all things.

5

The Mythic Quest

We notice that many learned and recondite writers whose work requires
patient study are explicitly mythopoeic writers.

Northrop Frye, *Anatomy of Criticism*

M ANDIARGUES'S FICTION is an accomplished, skillfully blended, and
learned amalgam of symbolic references and hidden allusions. An
introductory study of this nature can only point out some of its
more important ramifications. One level of his work which requires more
comment than most others (and which it will take two chapters to examine) is the mythical one. We know that *La Motocyclette* may be seen as
depicting the descent of a mythical heroine into the underworld. But the
descent into Hell is just one variation of a journey described in nearly all
myth, and this journey is also the basis of most of Mandiargues's fiction.
His work may be seen as a reconstruction of the archetypal myth, pursued
consistently, relentlessly, and with subtlety through novels, short stories,
and even critical works.

In his seminal work on myth, *The Hero with a Thousand Faces*,
Joseph Campbell describes the typical mythical journey. If we compare
Mandiargues's works to this description, we find that they follow an almost identical pattern. The journey of myth begins, for example, with a
"call to adventure." This is the call that Sigismond receives when his
cousin requests that he replace him in Barcelona. In *La Motocyclette* it
takes the form of a dream from which Rebecca awakes convinced that she
must set out to find Daniel. Sometimes, Campbell says, the journey
begins with an almost accidental call that comes as one is "casually strolling, when some passing phenomenon catches the wandering eye and
lures one away from the frequented paths of man."[1] These words strongly
recall the experience of Pascal Bénin, the main character in "Les Pierreuses" (*Feu de braise*), who, strolling in the country, hears a noise from
inside a stone, picks it up, and thus sets out on an adventure ending in his
death.

The hero of myth often receives the visit of a messenger, who

49

presents him with the call, and may accompany him as a guide. The messenger is usually an alluring female and she is surrounded by "an atmosphere of irresistible fascination." We have already encountered several such messengers in Mandiargues's fiction: the woman who lures Captain Idalium to his death in "L'Opéra des falaises" *(Soleil des loups)* and who is described as a "strangely unusual creature"; the figure who appears beside the narrator of "Le passage Pommeraye" *(Le Musée noir)* and whose haunting beauty he cannot resist; the prostitute whom Denis uses in "La Grotte" *(Porte dévergondée)* when he embarks on his dream journey, and who serves as "support, instrument, and guide." One might add to these the beautiful Flavia, one of Ferréol Buq's conquests, who rows him, like Charon, across a lake to a strange island.

The messenger of myth, according to Campbell, "is often dark, loathly, or terrifying, judged evil by the world." This description clearly fits the messengers of Mandiargues's fiction too. The woman in "Le passage Pommeraye" is deliberately linked to darkness and the night through the description of her black hair. The woman who lures away Captain Idalium also has black hair, and is dressed in black. Both women are, despite their fascinating beauty, sinister and frightening presences. The old man who guides Ferréol to the hill town also plays the role of guide (for this apparition need not always be female). He, although not strikingly evil, is clearly a disturbing and unusual figure. The solemn, ceremonial clothes that he wears, his great age, and his indeterminate sex make him seem like a creature from another time or dimension.

The call comes amidst an air of expectation, a feeling that something removed from man's normal experience is about to happen. Ferréol senses that some revelation, some deep secret is about to be revealed as he approaches the arena where the death ceremony is celebrated. In "L'Archéologue," a story in *Soleil des loups*, nature itself seems to anticipate some shattering event as Conrad Mur sits looking at the ocean. The trees and bushes stir, although there is no wind; a heavy silence falls, and the world seems to hold its breath. The atmosphere in which the messenger appears in "Le passage Pommeraye" from *Le Musée noir* is charged with anticipation of mysteries about to be revealed, a sense that an opening is about to be made in the usual fabric of reality. Omens of his fate appear to the narrator: the huge balloon in the sky above him (part of the 14 July celebrations) makes him think of "a propitiatory victim"; he sees a glove-maker's sign consisting of a red hand, its index finger raised as though in warning; the phrase "the burden of fate" comes into his head; he notices in one of the dusty windows such items as "Satan's fluid" and "murderer's soap"; when he follows the woman into a nearby street, he sees that it is called "rue de la Fosse" ("Street of the Grave"); then a train passes, carrying cattle to the slaughterhouse.

In "Les Pierreuses" from *Feu de braise,* Pascal Bénin, as he approaches the stone that will seal his fate, also encounters signs and omens. The phrase "It's cold enough to crack stones" recurs like an obsessive warning in his head. When he picks up the stone, some crows (often considered birds of evil omen) fly into the air, forming an M-shape. As Mandiargues points out, an M is used in Italy as an abbreviation for the expression "death to . . ." Then there is the case of Rebecca, who, during the course of her journey, is accompanied by a variety of "signs" pointing the way: road signs, directional signs, and traffic signals.[2]

Omens indicate that the hero has been chosen by forces beyond his ken, and he is now obliged to set out on a perilous quest. In *La Motocyclette* Rebecca Nul, like the knight of legend, leaves the safety of her home, the dull life of routine represented by her husband, and seeks adventure. Her similarity to the knight is deliberately underlined, for her motorcycle is referred to as "her mount" and as a "harnessed steed," while she herself, because of her black leather costume, is called "a knight in armor." She has to make an effort of will to face the journey, but, once this is done, she has only scorn for the people whose houses she passes, people who have not received the call and who sleep peacefully.

Rebecca, and the other characters like her, once they have set out, proceed to what Campbell calls "the threshold of adventure." Like the hero of myth, they have to cross thresholds, pass significant barriers, and go beyond points of no return. Rebecca crosses an international frontier and goes over several bridges spanning rivers. Sigismond Pons also crosses an international frontier when he goes to Spain, as does Vanina on her way to Italy. The idea of passage beyond a significant point is conveyed in the very title of "Le passage Pommeraye." These thresholds are, as in myth, kept by a guardian. The customs official in *La Motocyclette* plays the role of the gatekeeper to the underworld, and, on a previous journey, Rebecca and her lover had to pass a guardian in the form of the motel clerk who gave them the key to their room. He too was a sinister figure: emotionless, silent, and possibly dumb. The carabinieri whom Vanina fears she may meet in the night and who would prevent her going into the wood can be placed in the same category of uncooperative and probably dangerous watchmen.

The threshold guardian of myth is often a monstrous or half-animal creature. Captain Idalium has to pass a whole group of such figures as he enters the cave: devil-like animals who are playing a game that involves attaching rubber hoses to their penises. In some myths, it is the god Pan who is the "dangerous presence dwelling just beyond the protected zone."[3] On one of the journeys to her lover in *La Motocyclette,* Rebecca has to confront two customs men whose green uniforms make her think of foliage. Mandiargues writes: "One might classify them as conveniently in the vegetable realm as in the human species." Bearing in mind Pan's close links with the natural world, one may see his symbolic presence in these two men.

In order to pass the watchmen, the mythical hero has to answer a riddle or provide the solution to a puzzle. It is only after answering the frontier guard's questions about her identity and the money she is carrying that Rebecca is allowed to proceed. The papers that she shows him may be taken as symbolic of the talisman or charm which, in many myths, enables the hero to survive his ordeals. Since she has little money, Rebecca offers to leave her watch with the guard as earnest of her intent to return. One may see in this incident a reminder that the guardian, and especially the ferryman of death, usually required a fee. (The motel clerk actually is paid a small amount before giving the key to Rebecca and Daniel.) Akin to such puzzles and fees are the rites of passage that the hero has to perform, and which are recaptured in certain rituals of primitive societies: puberty rites, initiation into manhood, marriage, and birth rites. We have already discussed the role of ritual in Mandiargues's work, so little need be said here, except to recall that the loss of virginity is a common rite of passage in his fiction. Rebecca, Sarah, Vanina, and Marceline all undertake a passage into womanhood, and this is accompanied by ritual and by the spilt blood that is the visible sign of passage.

The next stage in the typical mythical journey is the crossing of a perilous wilderness where trials and ordeals must be suffered. This may be a desert, an enchanted wood, or a dark forest (a wilderness such as may be found in the forest of various Arthurian tales, in Dante's *selva oscura,* and in the desert to which Jesus retired to undergo trials by Satan). In Mandiargues's work, the desert is somewhat less exotic, and the ordeal consists simply of crossing it. Captain Idalium is led along a part of the seashore covered with slimy marine vegetation, rotting shell fish, and rusting metal. Ferréol Buq crosses a dense forest and a desert. Vanina, when she goes to meet the man in the wood, passes stagnant pools full of dead wood and bones, crosses an area of sewage, and then has to pick her way through a marsh full of branches, old planks, broken casks, and other rubbish that Mandiargues describes in *Le Lis de mer* as "the perilous region." In *La Motocyclette,* there are several references to a very famous crossing of the desert. Rebecca compares the trees receding in her rear view mirror to the Red Sea closing behind the children of Israel, and she thinks of Heidelberg, where her lover is, as Canaan.

During this dangerous part of the journey, the hero is sometimes given aid by a protective figure. In the case of Rebecca in *La Motocyclette,* Daniel is this figure, since it was he who, by giving her the motorcycle and teaching her how to ride it, provided her with the means to come to him. It was also he who taught her "the customs of the tavern, no less learnedly than the piloting of fast motorcycles." The liqueur that she pauses to drink in a café may, therefore, be seen as the equivalent of the magic potion that the protective power sometimes gives to the hero. In *La Marge*, Sigismond is accompanied and comforted by the memory of his wife, who becomes the directing and protective force. The prostitute whom he hires, by helping him hold death at bay, is another such figure, while the bottle of liqueur that seals the fatal letter is a kind of talisman against death.

So far, the journey undertaken by Mandiargues's characters corresponds in every stage to the typical mythical quest. When they reach the end of that quest, the similarity remains, for both journeys have the same goal. First, we must examine the female characters and see how they compare to the heroine of myth when they come to the end of their travels. In myth, the heroine (who is frequently a goddess herself) usually achieves union with a male deity when she arrives at the place she has been seeking. (Psyche seeks out and is united with Cupid, Isis with Osiris, and, in the Christian myth, the Virgin ascends to the bridal chamber of Heaven at the Feast of the Assumption.) As Campbell puts it: "When the adventurer . . . is not a youth but a maid, she is the one who, by her qualities, her beauty, or her yearning, is fit to become the consort of an immortal."[4] This "immortal" is a solar god, while the heroine is frequently associated with the moon.

As we know, Rebecca's journey in *La Motocyclette* recreates the descent of the goddess into the underworld in search of her male consort. Daniel, the goal of her quest, may, therefore, be compared to the solar deity. In the dream that sets her off on her journey, she is lying in a tree, like a flower "opening out and offering itself to the sun." Later in the journey, she twice stretches out in the sun to rest, offering herself, as it were, to its rays. Since her journey takes her eastwards, towards the rising sun, the solar being is the power that draws her. Her lover's full name is Daniel Lionart—both names that suggest lions, and the lion is a solar animal "found as a symbol of sun gods such as Mithras."[5] In fact, Mandiargues draws our attention to this, for he says in *Le Désordre de la mémoire:* "Daniel . . . is solar, as is indicated by the lion references in his name." As it happens, near where Daniel lives, is the site of an ancient temple to Mithras, and Rebecca's motorcycle is compared to a bull, an animal sacred to this diety. (The bull is also a symbol of Osiris, a deity sought out in the underworld by the lunar goddess Isis.)[6]

In several passages of the novel, Daniel is compared explicitly to a deity. Rebecca thinks of him as a "tiger god" and refers to his "having the look of a superior being." The color red, a solar color, is also associated with him. The room where he becomes Rebecca's lover is suffused in a red light, and his motorcycle is painted brilliant red. When Rebecca dies,

Daniel becomes the solar deity Bacchus. Her mind is full of thoughts of Daniel when she sees the face of Bacchus on the truck, and the two images seem to merge in her mind. In her death, she is finally united with the god who is the object of her quest.

Like Rebecca, Vanina in *Le Lis de mer* is associated with the female deity, in this case Isis. When she sees a statue of the Virgin and Child in the house where she is staying, she immediately compares it mentally to Isis and the Infant Horus. She herself is described as "a little Egyptian dancer carved in wood or ivory." She is linked to white, the goddess's color, by her white bathing suit and by her love of the white lilies that grow on the seashore. She also has an affinity with the moon, and plays the role of the lunar goddess in search of the sun god. The moon shines on her when she sets out to meet the man, and it is beneath the moon that she gives herself to him. At that moment, she feels " a kind of essential analogy" with the moon. On the way to her lover, she sees a large black pig, for which she feels "a kind of tenderness of a deep, almost fraternal kind." The pig too was associated with the moon goddess, and especially with Persephone.

Vanina's journey into the night to meet her lover is also a reenactment of the descent to the underworld. This interpretation is reinforced by other mythical references, such as the one to "a curtain of tamarisk" that Vanina has to push aside when she enters the wood. In Egyptian myth, Isis, hunting for Osiris in the underworld, found his body in a tamarisk tree. Vanina later leaves her shoes near a log that reminds her of a crocodile, and, in Egypt, the crocodile was sacred to Set, who abducted and killed Osiris.

The man whom Vanina meets in the wood must represent the male deity. He is implicitly compared to the god of the Old Testament when Vanina says: "I would like to be loved by the Lord, like the prophet Elisha in times past." More specifically, he is the solar deity. One of the things that induced Vanina to visit Sardinia was a pair of earrings shaped like a cock that a friend had brought back from the island. The cock, in many myths, is a solar symbol.[7] When she enters the wood, Vanina sees a bull, which, as we know, is also associated with the solar deity. The afternoon before she gives herself to the man, the sun shining on the wall of her room produces a kind of hallucination or dream of a red lion placing its paw on a naked girl, while a line of other girls, their hands tied behind their backs and their heads shaven, wait to take their turn. Vanina realizes, with her usual instinctive grasp of secret things, that the dream represents lunar maidens sacrificed to the sun.

Vanina will become one of these maidens, for she too is a worshipper of the sun. When we first meet her, she is stretched out on the beach, basking in its rays, and, in an erotic gesture that foreshadows her later union with the sun god, "she . . . parted her legs in order to offer them to the sun." She has, at this point, covered herself with oil, the kind of ritual anointment that a priestess might undergo.

A third heroine who must also receive a brief mention is Sarah Mose. In "Le Diamant" *(Feu de braise)*, Mandiargues recreates the myth of the pure virgin fecundated by a solar god. We are familiar with this myth through its biblical version of the Virgin Mary who conceives of the Holy Ghost.[8] Like Mary, Sarah is a Jewish virgin. The naked man is a sun god, since he resembles a lion and he is born of the sun's rays. From their union, as from the one described in the Bible, will be born a savior of Sarah's race.

Mandiargues's heroines are, in nearly every detail, comparable to the maid of myth who achieves union with the deity. But many of his characters are men, and cannot be fitted into exactly the same pattern. In their case, the goal of the mythical quest is somewhat different, and the version of the myth that Mandiargues recreates is a more primitive and basic one. Campbell describes the purpose of this ancient myth: "The ultimate adventure, when all the barriers and ogres have been overcome, is commonly represented as a mystical marriage of the triumphant hero-soul with the Queen Goddess of the world." We must, at this point, explain what is meant by the "Queen Goddess," before examining her presence in Mandiargues's work.

Behind much of the world's mythology is the figure of a mother goddess. Most myth has its origin at a time and place in which "the focal point of all mythology and worship was the bountiful goddess Earth, as the mother and nourisher of life and the receiver of the dead for rebirth."[9] She represents the generative powers of the earth and of the female, their birth-giving and nourishing function. She is the mother of the universe, but also the giver of death. She is Aphrodite, Isis, Venus, the mother goddess of the Cretans, and even the Mother of God in the Christian myth.

This deity was dethroned toward the end of the Bronze Age when the matriarchal agricultural society that produced her was subjected to incursions from patriarchal warrior groups. The mythology of these warriors and hunters was based on a male solar deity (the one whose presence we have already detected in several of Mandiargues's pieces of fiction). The new deity (whose influence is best seen in the Judao-Christian myth and in the gods of Greece) replaced the old goddess, who was now given a dark and fearful aspect. The male deity was taken as representing all that was good, heroic, and noble. His victory represented the triumph of light over darkness, since he was a solar god, and the goddess was linked to the powers of night and to the moon. Yet the influence of the goddess persisted, and she can still be seen in somewhat altered form in later myths.

She is the dark forces worshipped in the mystery cults of Greece; she is Pallas Athene, Medusa, and Circe. The dust from which Adam was created is probably a residual memory of the earth mother. In Christianity, her powers as the dark force of nature became associated with Satan.[10]

Mandiargues, for his part, is well aware of the importance of the mother goddess in myth. When describing the oven in which Miró made his ceramic figures, he says in *Troisième Belvédère* that it has a maternal appearance, "like nature, or more precisely, the earth, in most primitive mythologies." He sees the presence of the goddess in much of the fiction of fantasy produced by English, Welsh, and Irish writers. He says that the works of Yeats, Graves, Machen, Saki, and Crowley all show "a persistence of the old panic, nature religion, the religion of the Germanic Wotan, of the horned god and of the mighty mother goddess (the great mother, the great goddess), exiled . . . by God the Father, the Avenger, otherwise known as the God whom the Jews bequeathed to the Christians."[11] Once more, Mandiargues's insight into the works of others is just as much an insight into his own.

To illustrate this point, our best example is a short story that we have not yet examined in any detail: "L'Archéologue" from *Soleil des loups*. This is one of Mandiargues's longer works, more of a *nouvelle* than a short story, and it contains his usual mixture of extraordinary events and symbolic references. It tells of Conrad Mur, a cold and studious young archaeologist who dislikes contact with women because their warm, living bodies remind him of death and decay. He avoids all sexual adventure, all passion, and lives a rather dreary, dusty life. One winter, while staying with his mother in Switzerland, he goes skating on a frozen lake where the villagers have organized a carnival. Although disgusted by the alcoholic and sexual excesses of these people, he is attracted to a cold and statuesque girl who singles him out and asks him to skate with her. Shortly after, he becomes engaged to her, and, in the summer, he takes her to Italy. Here they meet a rather sinister priest called the abbé Mercurio, who shows them a wax figure that he keeps in a specially designed room. It represents a young girl, her stomach cut open, and a mass of strawberries pouring from the open wound. Both Conrad and Bettina, his fiancée, are strangely troubled by this sight, and Bettina falls ill soon afterwards. Conrad, sickened by her suffering, which makes her a much less cold and sexless creature, abandons her to an unkempt, lecherous doctor and makes for the coast. Here, as he sits watching the ocean, he is transported in a dream to the sea bed, where he encounters a monstrous statue wearing the ring that he had given Bettina. That night, in a natural arena, he meets the same figure, followed by a horde of toads or frogs. It strips off its clothes, then releases the frogs, which set upon Conrad and kill him.

The critical scene in "L'Archéologue" is the descent beneath the sea, which is also the opening scene. (The rest of the story, with the exception of Conrad's final encounter with the monstrous figure, is told as a flashback.) It happens amidst the usual air of expectation, an atmosphere pregnant with mysteries about to be revealed. Once on the sea bed, Conrad has to pass through an area of mud, slime, and decaying fish that one may liken to the mythical wilderness crossed by most heroes. Then he sees "a large statue of a woman that reared its heavy nakedness in his path, sculpted in green, almost black marble." The blackness of the figure links her at once to the earth goddess, who represented dark, hidden forces. Her expression is "among the most bestial," for the deity is animal-like and close to the world of nature. That she is the deity of fertility is clear from the gestures she makes: "One arm is held around an empty space, as though to embrace a voluptuous partner; the other points a hand downwards, indicating with an inviting gesture her lower stomach." The coral encrusted on her head forms "a diadem of tiny horns," and one can easily make the link between this and the horns of the moon. Conrad Mur, who is, after all, an archaeologist, recognizes in this statue "a figure of the Great Venus Meretrix." Venus, of course, is just one form that the earth mother took.

This dreamlike encounter is one of three made by Conrad with the female deity. The wax figure that he is shown earlier is the first of them, and the abbé Mercurio may be seen as the messenger/guide who leads him to the goal of his quest.[12] The figure is kept in a kind of shrine, on the windows of which are blinds bearing figures holding clubs and tridents. The trident is associated with Satan's fork, and Satan represents the dark, underground side of the goddess. The wax statue itself, with the fruit pouring from her body, is the goddess in her aspect as the fecund, female giver of life. But Conrad also senses something powerfully malignant in her. It is his fate always to meet the dangerous side of the deity, and he relizes that the fruit issuing from her are "fruit from a garden of Hell, rooted in living flesh and luxuriantly demoniac."

The climax of the story comes when Conrad meets the goddess for the third time and she unleashes her hostile force on him. In the usual ritual setting, he sees a dark, tall figure whom he immediately associates with the statue on the sea bed. She slowly discards her clothes, in a kind of religious cleansing rite that recalls Sarah Mose's stripping and washing. As the clothes fall to the ground, they disappear in smoke, yet another sign that she is a deity, since fire and smoke are often signs of the divine presence (as, for example, in the story of Moses and the burning bush). Conrad knows that he is facing a supernatural being, that "she. . . . is not part of the usual order of men and women." He realizes that her strange, unseeing eyes are another sign of this, for "such impenetrable airs as these always conceal gods who have taken on human shape to deceive men." The frogs who surround her and the unusually bright moon in the sky indicate that she incarnates the forces of nature.

Conrad Mur does not achieve union with the deity. He, by his life of sexual abstemiousness, has rejected the female deity, and she punishes him by death. Pascal Bénin in *Les Pierreuses (Feu de braise)* undergoes a similar fate, for he too is a dry-as-dust scholar who gives no thought to the female presence in life. The three tiny figures whom he releases from the stone are versions of the goddess, for they inform him that they are *egressae ex utero magnae matris nostrae*. Pascal immediately realizes that this is a reference to "nature, for example the great goddess of Asia, or a (female) personification of the elemental fire." They disappear in flames and cause Pascal's death.[13]

In some stories the bestial side of the goddess is particularly emphasized. The woman who guides the narrator of "Le passage Pommeraye" *(Le Musée noir)* is an avatar of the goddess. The only word she says to him is "Echidna"—but it is a significant word. In ancient mythology, Echidna was half serpent, half woman, so the figure in this story may be identified with the female deity in her animal-like aspect. This is reinforced by a reference to her "good animal smell." Her association with serpents is also important, for the serpent was linked to the earth mother (who appears, in this guise, in the Garden of Eden myth). The woman's black hair is a further reference to a deity who incarnates the dark powers of the universe.

The bestial aspect of the deity is also emphasized in "Adive" from *Mascarets*. The girl whom Stéphanie follows is another avatar of the goddess, and has obvious animal connotations. She refers to her apartment, for example, as "my den." Once they arrive there, the girl disappears, and Stéphanie can find only a dog in the apartment. It is as though the girl has become the dog, which, by caressing Stéphanie, produces a sexual climax. This may be seen as a kind of union with the deity. It is also interesting to note that, near where Stéphanie first meets the girl, there was once a temple of Isis—yet another of the forms taken by the earth mother.

Even "Le Marronnier," (also from *Mascarets*), behind its intellectual games and its speculation about time, tells in symbolic form of a hero's union with the mother goddess. Throughout the conversation on time, Jean de Lugio is wishing that the other man would leave so that he may be alone to make love to the woman. The latter is called Cérès, which is the name of the Roman goddess of wheat, harvests, and fertility; in other words, the earth mother. The tree under which they sit during their discussion may be seen as the Tree of Life. In many myths, the tree represents the world navel from which the life forces, personified by the goddess, radiate.[14] Because it represents life, the tree is often associated with sexual forces, as is the goddess herself. It is little surprise, then, when Mandiargues describes this tree as having a "perfume of sexual effusion." When the story ends, and the other man has left, we are led to believe that Jean de Lugio will attain the desired union with Cérès.[15]

In "Le Marronnier" and other stories mentioned here, Mandiargues uses the goddess's name (Cérès, Echidna), or indicates by other means that he is referring to her. But the goddess of myth is merely the symbol or incarnation of forces that need not necessarily be expressed in this form. In ancient myth, the forces of life frequently appear in their pure form, unpersonified as a goddess. Mandiargues too chooses, in some of his fiction, to show these powers in this light. In so doing, he comes very close to ancient, pre-Christian myth in his view of the deity.

Primitive and Eastern myth differ from the great religions of the West in that, for them, the deity is not transcendent, but immanent.[16] The great goddess, who lies at the heart of this mythology, is the personification of life forces that are conceived of as being everywhere in creation, both in man and in the world surrounding him. Christianity sees God as the creator of the world, but does not see him as *in* the world. The Christian god can manifest himself only in special revelation: on Sinaï, in the burning bush, in the form of Christ. But the deity of the earliest myths is in all things—indeed, *is* all things. At its most primitive, this belief is found in worship of magic forces in nature; at its most sophisticated, in Indian Buddhist and in Vedantic thought. The arrival of the solar deity in the West changed much of this belief. The side of the female deity that was seen as immanent in the world around man was now depicted as dark and dangerous. These forces were associated with certain frightening deities. Pan, whose appearances throw the beholder into panic, came to represent these forces insofar as they were manifested in the natural world. In Christianity, the divine power in the world became associated with Satan.

It is with the divine forces inherent in creation that Mandiargues's characters achieve contact in their moments of erotic ecstasy, and he even uses the name of Pan in order to describe them. Rebecca, Vanina, and Marceline are united with the very forces of creation in their natural form, without need for personification or borrowing the form of a deity. When they unite with their lovers, the "panic" communion that they feel with nature is communion with the forces of the divine in creation. Through their partners, they become one with the divine that ancient myth sees all around us. The signs and omens are merely other ways in which the forces show themselves and beckon on Mandiargues's heroes and heroines. These characters, like the mythical hero, become the instruments of powers beyond their ken and are led on until, at the end of their quest, they encounter these powers in a moment of "mystical marriage."

Mandiargues often uses Christian terminology and describes the powers in nature as dark and evil. He points out that they frequently are seen in demons and witches, and he writes: "Witches are also female incarnations of the great force or the great spirit of universal nature, and this links them to ancient panic traditions."[17] He believes that particular places seem more imbued with the dark forces than others, and one such site is Palenque in Mexico, where, he says in *Deuxième Belvédère*, something "Luciferian" may be felt. Certain artists are especially aware of this side of creation, and Mandiargues praises Chirico in *Troisième Belvédère* for saying that the artist must capture "the demon that lies hidden in the depths of every being and every thing." Bettencourt, Landolfi, and Gambini are among those who have done this. He also finds in Milton, Blake, Maturin, and Lautréamont a taste for "the dark underside of creation" and talks of their "affection given to the evil side of the universe."[18]

In his own fiction, when these powers reveal themselves, they are often dark too. Marceline feels the forces of night all around her as she leaves her parents' house, and these forces are incarnated by the black shepherd whom she meets. The powers that Conrad Mur senses in the wax figure are devilish and the goddess figures who appear in "Le passage Pommeraye," "L'Archéologue," and "L'Opéra des falaises" are all dark in appearance. Even the term "panic" applied to the forces encountered in moments of erotic ecstasy indicates that they are linked to the dark deity Pan.

Whatever form these powers take and whether dark or solar, Mandiargues's characters always encounter them during their journeys. However they are depicted, they are the same divine forces that the hero of myth finds at the end of his quest. To express his view of life and of man's relation to the forces of life, Mandiargues has gone back to the earliest conception of existence that man has ever held. He has returned to a time when man lived close to the world, when he knew instinctively that there were forces in it that "civilized" man can no longer feel. With humor, erudition, and clever manipulation of symbols and mythical references, he has woven this view of life into his novels and stories. The scope of these mythical references has only been lightly touched on here, and one more chapter must be devoted to a few more of their ramifications.

6

The Uses of Myth

Tout porte à croire qu'il existe un certain point de l'esprit d'où la vie et la mort, le réel et l'imaginaire, le passé et le futur, le communicable et l'incommunicable, le haut et le bas, cessent d'être perçus contradictoirement.
André Breton, *Second manifeste du surréalisme*

OF THE SEVERAL OTHER POINTS OF CONTACT between Mandiargues's fiction and myth, the one that most readily strikes the reader is the dreamlike atmosphere of nearly everything that he has written. Characters evolve and events take place in a world where the laws of waking reality no longer hold true, and we have the impression that we are in a trance, a dream, or, in some tales, a nightmare. This aspect of his fiction will be examined in more detail later, but it should be mentioned here as one of the elements that link it to myth. As Jung has pointed out, the happenings and symbols of myth often appear in dreams too, and myth itself may be seen as a kind of collective dream. Mankind seems spontaneously to produce in its recurring myths the same symbols and events as in its dreams. Consequently, myth often resembles dream, and what strikes us as dreamlike in Mandiargues's fiction may also be seen, in another light, as typically mythical.

The characters who live these dreams are also best viewed as mythical beings. They are not "realistic" in the tradition of the nineteenth-century novel, and they certainly do not have the psychological depth and complexity of a Julien Sorel or an Emma Bovary. Rebecca and Vanina do have some traits that individualize them and give them life as distinctive human beings. Rebecca is a sensuous creature, avidly interested in the world around her and an endearing mixture of timidity and daring; Vanina is a self-willed young woman, as willing as Rebecca to flout conventional attitudes, and immensely curious about the world and life. Yet even these two, the most individual of Mandiargues's characters, are not ones with whom one can consistently and unquestioningly identify.

As for the male characters, they are rarely living people whom one can know as one "knows" Julien Sorel, for example. Sigismond Pons is a colorless being who lives only through memories and events in which he is a helpless participant. Ferréol Buq has more life in him than Sigismond, but his cynical exploitation of women and his carefree attitudes merely bring him sporadically alive. In the short stories, the amount of character portrayal is necessarily limited by the length of the story, but even in short fiction, more attempt can be made to individualize and motivate characters. Only Conrad Mur, Sarah Mose, and Marceline Caïn have a spark of individualized life.

These remarks are not, of course, intended as an adverse comment on Mandiargues's work. There is no reason why a writer should adhere unthinkingly to nineteenth-century ideas of characterization if his goal is different from Flaubert's or Stendhal's. The fact is that Mandiargues has no intention of creating "realistic" people because he is attempting, not to analyze the human psyche or the complicated emotions of the heart, but to express other truths. His characters are epiphanies, vehicles of mythical forces, and, through them, Mandiargues tries to reveal man's relationship to the world in which he lives. Like the heroes of myth, they have to find their way in a world of unknown forces, and, by their lives and their experiences, they reveal these forces. They may be compared to participants in a ritual who have lost their sense of individuality. In primitive rituals, where ancient myths are brought alive for the benefit of members of the community at critical stages in their lives (puberty, marriage, etc.), the actors are no longer themselves. In any such ceremony, to quote Joseph Campbell, "the individuals rendering it are not individuals any more, but epiphanies of a cosmic mystery."[1] It is this "cosmic mystery" that Mandiargues uses his characters to reveal.

The events described are no more "realistic" than the characters to whom they happen: people shrink in size, are swallowed by precious stones, find themselves transported to the sea bed, and see the future happening before their eyes. Such fiction does not aim at being "convincing" in the usual sense of the word, and requires a willing suspension of disbelief. The reader has to have a kind of imaginative faith in the events described that is akin to primitive man's belief in myth. Neither the readers of these stories nor those who once listened to mythic tales necessarily accept that the events narrated are literally true, but rather that they stand for something else. One must take Mandiargues's fiction as men took myth, as an image of a deeper mystery. Both are figurative representations of man's position in the world and of the nature of that world.

Even the settings of Mandiargues's works have a distinctly mythical character. Although they may seem at first reading to be very specific, and although they are often described in great detail, they still have something vague and timeless about them. "Le passage Pommeraye" is

set in an actual street in Nantes, but this street is transformed into something nightmarish and mysterious that defies location. Sigismond Pons
walks in a district of Barcelona that really exists, past bars and cinemas
that are named and described minutely, yet this is also a world set *en
marge*, a world that exists nowhere in particular and where time has no
meaning. Ferréol Buq travels in Italy, but it is an Italy of secret towns,
strange ceremonies, and mysterious old buildings that appear in no tour-
ist brochure nor on any map. Rebecca rides through named towns and her
journey follows a clearly demarcated route that may be followed on a
map, but her real journey takes place inside her, in a *terrain vague*
between memories, longings, and spurts of intense desire. Like myth
itself, these stories are set in a location that is deliberately imprecise so
that it may refer to any time and any place. Myth is not localized, but
evolves in an unknown setting where anyone may feel at home. Much of
its appeal is due to the absence of specific spatial references that may
remove it from the individual's experience.

Nor is myth localized in time, and, here again, we find one very
important link with Mandiargues's fiction. We have already said that
Mandiargues tries to defy time and to create a world in which temporal
categories may be ignored. This is particularly evident in *La Marge* and
La Motocyclette, where he evokes a period in which time stands still.
Myth too has a timeless quality, for it is set outside of history as we know
it. It takes place at a time before time began and is valid for all men in all
ages. To quote Mircea Eliade: "As is generally admitted today, a myth is
an account of events which took place *in principio*, that is, 'in the beginning,' in a primordial and non-temporal instant, a moment of *sacred
time*."[2] Mandiargues's fiction also "takes man out of his own time—his
individual, chronological 'historic' time—and projects him, symbolically
at least, into the Great Time, into a paradoxical instant which cannot be
measured because it does not consist of duration."[3] We are moved, as it
were, from our historical situation to a higher reality, a plane of eternal
truths that knows no beginning nor end.

Myth in general is timeless, but the instant of union with the
deity is especially and invariably removed from temporal flow. It is set in
"an instant without duration, as certain mystics and philosophers conceived of eternity."[4] The deity is beyond all temporal categories, eternal.
In French, God is called "L'Eternel" (which is also the term that Vanina
uses when referring to him in *Le Lis de mer*), and in the Bible we read: "I
am Alpha and Omega, the beginning and the ending, saith the Lord,
which is, and which was, and which is to come, the Almighty" (Rev. I : 8).
As all mystics declare, union with the deity is release from temporal
bonds, so it is not surprising that this moment in Mandiargues's works is
set beyond time. We can now see one more reason why the instant of

"panic" communion is one in which watches, clocks, and all references to time are abolished.

There are, scattered through the stories and novels, several other signs frequently encountered in myth that indicate when the heroes and heroines are in the presence of a divine power. One of these, which we have noted before, is the tree, which appears in "Le Marronnier," "La Grotte," and "L'Archéologue." The tree represents the center of the universe in myth, and it is precisely at this center that the deity is to be found.[5] Another such symbol of the center is the menhir, and Ferréol Buq passes several of these as he approaches the arena where he receives enlightenment.[6]

In other stories, characters have to find their way through a maze before reaching their goal. Rebecca has to negotiate a labyrinth of streets in the town where Daniel lives, and there is an obvious allusion to the minotaur myth when Mandiargues writes in La Motocyclette that Rebecca "was guided as though by a thread that Daniel was pulling." In La Marge, the prostitutes' quarter is described as having a maze of streets, and another district of the city is "one of those little labyrinths common to all central city areas in the world." These references are not accidental, for the maze figures widely in myth. It represents symbolically the internal organs of the female and the path to the womb. To travel to its center is, therefore, to travel to the center of life, to the place where dwells the goddess of life.[7] The maze is also a protective device to keep unwelcome intruders away from the deity, and only the hero who has divine guidance may successfully negotiate it.

The spiral plays much the same role in myth as the maze: it protects the deity and is normally found at the point where the divine forces are present.[8] Not surprisingly, spirals are a common feature of Mandiargues's work. The narrator of "Le Marronnier" (Mascarets) hopes to take Cérès to a room at the top of a spiral staircase. The tomb that opens and swallows the characters in "Armoire de lune" (Mascarets) descends in a double spiral; the narrator of "Le passage Pommeraye" (Le Musée noir) follows his guide up a spiral staircase; the chamber where Sarah Mose examines the diamond is at the head of a similar stairway.

Mandiargues's interest in spirals and mazes is just part of a wider fascination with geometric designs and symmetrical figures. In an article called "L'Espion des Pouilles" from Le Cadran lunaire, he writes with obvious interest of the strangely symmetrical Castel del Monte in Italy, while articles like "La cité métaphysique," from the same volume, and "Certains visionnaires" (Deuxième Belvédère) talk of geometric shapes in the work of Bosch and Giorgio Morandi. Rebecca rides along roads that intersect at angles, describe curves, and progress in arcs, and she keeps her cycle between the parallel lines of the fast lane on the highway. But it is mainly in the ritual scenes that the obsession with geometry is most obvious, in the carefully selected natural arenas, the antique temples, the symmetrical rooms, and the geometrically intricate dances and ceremonials that surround various characters' meetings with the life forces. There is a firmly established link in Mandiargues's mind between geometric shapes and the kind of frenzy that his characters display in their moments of sexual communion with the "panic" in nature. He comments in one of his essays in *Le Cadran lunaire* on "those links, those curious affinities, that one may observe between sites that are subject to the laws of geometry and uncontrolled, even frenzied states of the soul and the senses." It is no coincidence that he chose to set the erotic excesses of *L'Anglais décrit dans le château fermé* in a geometrically shaped castle.

The connection between geometric decor and delirious possession by powerful forces is well established in myth and ancient religion. The divine presence is frequently accompanied by some kind of geometric design or mandala. The mandala is a traditional device, found mainly in Hindu ritual, that is used to lead the mind toward the divinity. It consists of concentrically arranged figures, which, in Jung's words, "always show a specific pattern: they are circular or square, or like a cross or a star, or are composite of such elements."[9] An examination of the geometric designs in almost any of Mandiargues's fiction reveals that they too are mandalas.

The tiny goddesses who emerge from the stone when Pascal Bénin splits it open perform a geometric dance in which circles and triangles intersect and are superimposed on each other. Rebecca, as she lies in the room where she later communicates with the "panic" powers through Daniel, feels as though she is surrounded by the facets of a huge ruby. These facets form an intricate mandala of which she is the center. Sarah Mose, inside the diamond, is the center of a similar mandala, and Mandiargues dwells at some length on the geometric lines that could be drawn around the lion man: his outstretched hands and feet are the corners of a rectangle set within the polyhedron of the diamond, his navel forms the point of intersection of the diagonals of this figure, and his erect member is in the same proportion to his body as the number pi. In "Le Marronnier," the tree (where Cérès, the goddess, sits) forms the center of a circle made by the marijuana cigarette that the characters pass to one another. The characters themselves sit in a circle around the tree, and "the smokers' feet could form the roughly equidistant summits of a three-pointed star, the center of which would coincide with the tree." Around them is a circular lawn, then a ring of bushes, and the whole is enclosed in a square garden.

It is at the center of these figures that Rebecca, Sarah, and (probably) Jean de Lugio commune with the divine power that is the goal of their quest. This is as it should be, for, in Eastern religions, the middle of the mandala contains the deity. To quote Jung again: "In the very center of the mandala there is a god, or the symbol of divine energy, the diamond thunderbolt."[10] These geometric figures are not in Mandiargues's works by accident, but to indicate, as they do in myth, that the hero has found the source of divine energy, that he has reached the end of his search, and that he has been brought to that point where the obscure powers around him have been drawing him.

The mythical references and signs that we have so far noted—the dreamlike atmosphere, the use of characters as epiphanies, the manipulation of time, the type of setting, the mazes, spirals, and mandalas—are all there because Mandiargues wants to indicate that we are observing a mythic journey. He is telling us that his heroes, like the heroes of myth, have discovered a world in which there are mysterious forces that speak to them and lead them on to the point where they have their origin. When this point is reached, the heroes discover the nature of the forces, and Mandiargues's conception of their nature also corresponds closely with that of myth.

The forces of creation are often represented in myth, and in Mandiargues's fiction, as a female deity because the female form has always seemed to mankind to be the living embodiment of life itself. Woman is the beginning of life, the giver of birth, the sustainer and nourisher. The mysteries of the female body, its ability to give life and its cyclic rhythms all seemed to early men to mirror closely the marvels of nature, and the awe that they must have felt before it is reflected in Mandiargues's frequently expressed wonder at woman. "There can be no doubt," Campbell writes, "that in the very earliest ages of human history, the magical force and wonder of the female was no less a marvel than the universe itself."[11] Marriage with the deity represents the releasing of the power of life into the hero, and it is this release and renewal of life that Mandiargues's heroes achieve when they unite with the deity.

But Mandiargues also has a profoundly dualistic idea of life and of the forces that mold it. Here again, his instinctive grasp of the strangely paradoxical nature of life is identical with that of primitive man. Myth too depicts life in terms of linked opposites, and the goddess herself combines in her person all these opposites. She is the giver of life, but she is also death and the powers of decay. "She is the womb and the tomb: the sow that eats her farrow."[12] Pascal Bénin, Ferréol Buq, and others find that the forces of life can also destroy. In "L'Archéologue" (Soleil des loups) Conrad Mur discovers this truth in the person of the goddess herself. The statue that he encounters is obviously the deity in her sexual, life-giving nature, as she indicates by her erotic gesture. Conrad symbolically marries her by removing the ring from her finger and placing it on his own.

But he is foolish enough, the moment after, to reject her by putting it back on her finger. When he meets her again, she is a vengeful deity who metes out death to him.

The goddess assumes in her person the dual nature of existence by being simultaneously beautiful and ugly. This is why Conrad Mur is struck by both the heavy beauty and the barbaric ugliness of the statue. The woman who appears in "Le passage Pommeraye" is also, behind her alluring charm, an animal-like and somewhat ugly creature. Mandiargues realizes that deities often appear as monsters as well as in the form of beautiful beings, and he says in Troisième Belvédère that "in almost all religions gods and demons are presented to the faithful in the form of monstrous figures." These monstrous deities merely symbolize an elementary fact of life. Mandiargues writes in Le Belvédère: "Beauty is so closely linked to the beast that men have never been able to see the semblance of a monster or a dragon without imagining that it watched over Andromeda."

The sexual dualism that is so basic to Mandiargues's conception of existence is just as fundamental to myth. Most mythology assumes a time when there was no division between the sexes, when male and female coexisted in the same being. The original ancestor of mankind is frequently depicted as androgynous. (There are traces of this idea in the Judao-Christian myth, for, before the creation of Eve, she was part of Adam, who was, therefore, male and female.) The deity who created this original being often shares its male/female nature.[13] Even the great goddess contains within her the male sex. Certain of Mandiargues's heroes who seek the deity are also strongly androgynous: Rebecca, Sigismond, and Ferréol Buq. The avatars of the goddess who appear in the stories are often hermaphroditic too. Sigismond's wife, the girl who lures Stéphanie to her apartment, and the old man who guides Ferréol to the ceremony.

The varied strands of myth that we have examined in this chapter are drawn together in one curious and fascinating episode in Marbre which also shows Mandiargues at his best as a weaver of symbolic fantasy. Ferréol Buq persuades the young woman in whose house he stays for several days (and whom he seduces) to row him across a lake to an island that mysteriously draws him to it. It is with great reluctance that she plays the role of the mythical ferryman, for the island has an evil reputation. But the religious dread that emanates from it only attracts Ferréol all the more, for, like a true hero, he is always willing to leave the beaten track, to ignore taboos, and to search out secrets that others fear.

He discovers on this island a huge statue set in the midst of a ritualistic arrangement of monuments that form a mandala. There are five of them, shaped in the form of regular polyhedrons (a tetrahedron, a cube, an octahedron, a dodecahedron, and an icosahedron), and they constitute the five points of a pentagon. The statue is at the very center of this arrangement, occupying the place where the deity is always found. It is made of marble, eroded by time, and is about five or six hundred years old. It represents a colossal hermaphrodite, hollow inside, with skillfully disguised windows and a wooden ladder leading to the entrance.

Ferréol achieves a kind of sexual and mystic union with this deity by entering it through a door of which he says: "I could not in all modesty say where this door was located." He finds himself in the statue's dark, damp, and oppressive belly, and compares himself to another hero who descended into a mythical beast: Jonah. He then proceeds to the thorax, which is a well-lit room containing twenty-five pentagonal columns arranged symmetrically in a group. On these columns are painted scenes of torture, murder, blood, and frenzy—once again, orgy and destruction are linked to geometric patterns. When he reaches the head, he finds frescos representing what he calls "the triumph of delirium": madmen of all kinds converging on a naked, bestial, but strangely beautiful god. After that, he climbs on the statue's head and surveys the countryside.

Some nights later, Ferréol returns alone to the island. A full moon (symbol of the goddess) shines with supernatural brightness on the scene, and, remembering it many days afterwards as he lies on a beach, he opens his eyes and gazes at the sun (symbol of the male deity). These images—sun and moon, male and female—are superimposed in his mind as he recalls how he entered the statue and passed through the two rooms with the paintings in them. He moves symbolically in this scene through the kind of delirium associated with possession by the divine spirit, and finds himself again on the statue's head. All frenzy and desire are stilled within him as he seems to become part of the surrounding world. The wind blowing through the columns inside the statue produces a strange and harmonious sound that puts him in tune with the harmony of all. The monuments surrounding the statue appear transparent in the moonlight, and he is struck by the contrast between "the divine harmony of such a scene, and the images of blood and delirium through which, like initiation rites, I had had to pass before arriving at this superior point of view."

The statue combines within it, like the ancient goddess, all the contradictions of existence. By its hermaphrodite form, it symbolizes the unity behind the contradictions. When he enters it, Ferréol is able to pass beyond the delirium of divine possession and adopt the "superior point of view" of someone who has achieved enlightenment. He can now see the unity of all things, and this is the ultimate secret revealed by myth. Just as he can look through the monuments to their other side, he can see through the surface appearances of the world and comprehend its other, hidden side.

Ferréol is given one more demonstration of the unity of life (in this case, the unity of life and death) during the ceremony in the hill town. However, it seems likely that he dies later, and is unable to pass on the secrets that he has discovered. Sigismond, Rebecca, Conrad Mur, and several less important characters also die, so their discovery of the nature of existence remains a secret too. Marceline survives her experiences, but is sent to an orphanage where she seems to revert to her childlike behavior. Vanina survives unscathed, but the novel ends as she leaves Sardinia, so we never know what use she makes of her discoveries. The endings of Mandiargues's stories would appear to be the only point at which they depart from the archetypal myth, for the hero of myth usually returns from his quest with some gift or boon to bestow on other men. Like Theseus, he may have saved his people from an oppressive fate, or, like Jesus, he may have saved the whole of humanity. Sometimes, like Jason, he returns with a source of wealth and power. Only Sarah among Mandiargues's heroes and heroines seems more or less to fit this pattern, for she returns bearing inside her a child who will be a savior of his race.

There are, however, other adventurers involved in these stories besides the obvious heroes and heroines. The reader accompanies Rebecca on her quest and discovers with her the identity of life and death; he realizes, with Vanina, that the life forces are all around us and may be felt by anybody with the necessary will and sensitivity; he learns, as does Conrad Mur, that it is wrong and dangerous to ignore such forces; he sees through Ferréol Buq's eyes that all the contradictions of life hide a fundamental unity. After the story is read and the characters are dead, its resonances, discoveries, and ideas live on in the reader's mind. Mandiargues's characters do live long enough to reveal the secrets they have discovered, and it is to the reader that they give this boon. We are the hero's people to whom the secrets are revealed.

This does not mean that Mandiargues teaches a "lesson" or advocates a particular set of attitudes. He presents no all-embracing system for our edification, draws no dramatic conclusions, and points to no course of action that we must take. His art is not didactic in that sense. He merely attempts, as does myth itself,[14] to express the awe that all sensitive individuals feel before the mystery of being, to show us the hidden forces, the marvelous powers in the world around us, to show the forces of life hidden even in death. He tries to convey a typically mythical image of the universe as light and dark, life and death, good and evil, all bound together in an inextricable whole.

Such truths as these are not easy to grasp, and the returning hero of myth always has difficulty expressing them.[15] It is because they are inexpressible in ordinary speech that Mandiargues has recourse to symbolic language. Symbols are not the literal expression of truth, but convey something beyond themselves, something which often denies rational expression. "As the mind explores the symbol, it is led to ideas that lie beyond the grasp of reason" says Jung.[16] The irrational, paradoxical, complex, and marvelous nature of life can be expressed in no other way than in symbols. Since it is myth that deals most consistently and thoroughly with this paradoxical complexity, Mandiargues naturally arranges his symbols in mythical patterns.

7

The Journey Inwards

Quelle chimère est-ce donc que l'homme? Quelle nouveauté, quel mon-
stre, quel chaos, quel sujet de contradiction, quel prodige!

Pascal, *Pensées*

DREAMS AND REVERIE form the very warp and woof of Pieyre de
Mandiargues's fiction. They suffuse and underlie nearly all that he
has written, investing it with the hypnotic power that dreams have
always held over the human imagination. In scene after scene, his characters find themselves in a world far removed from the logic of commonplace reality. Time stops, the postulates of everyday life are suspended,
and events obey different laws. The mysterious passage in "Le passage
Pommeraye," the undersea world at the beginning of "L'Archéologue,"
the interior of the diamond in "Le Diamant," and even the streets of
Barcelona in *La Marge* are just a few of these oneiric locations, representing not so much an unreal world as one in which a new reality is created
and a new set of rules applied.

In some cases, whole stories are based on the premise (beloved of
the surrealists) that dream may extend into the normal world and take it
over. The woman in "Le Triangle ambigu" from *Mascarets* has a recurring
nightmare that finally affects her behavior and changes events: she refuses
to remain with the male character for fear of acting out her dream and
killing him. In "Le Songe et le métro," a story in *Sous la lame* a woman
deliberately goes to a Métro station that she has seen in her sleep, hoping
to make her dream come true. Marie Mors's visions of the future actually
do come true. Perhaps the best example of dream impinging on life is the
play *Isabella Morra*. The heroine of this work, who lives in a poetic dream
where she loves and is loved by Diego Sandoval, refuses to deny her
brothers' accusations that this man is her lover. Rather than admit that
she has never met him, she upholds the right of dreams, clings to poetic
fiction, and dies for them.

Mandiargues is, of course, proud that dreams lie at the basis of
his work. He has admitted in *Le Désordre de la mémoire:* "But I believe

71

that my work in its entirety is a kind of great dream or vast reverie,"
adding that his first published poem, *Hedera,* "comes directly from dream
and reverie." He has said: "My dreams are sometimes infernal, sometimes heavenly, but it is from them that I draw almost all the substance of
my writings."[1] In one interview, he says that in order to write he has to be
in "a state that must be nourished by dream."[2] Literature in general, he
claims in *Le Cadran lunaire,* is dream set down on paper: "It is an old idea
of mine that a book, an essay, a poem or a narrative work is nothing in fact
but a reverie (meditation) that is more or less directed, prolonged (sometimes for a whole lifetime) as much as seems necessary, supported by
verbal rhythm (style), fixed in black and white by the instruments of ink
and paper." An article in *Troisième Belvédère* defines the novel as "a
dream plucked out of flux" and the novelist as "an inspired dreamer."

Dreams have been an essential part of Mandiargues's life as well
as of his art. In *Le Désordre de la mémoire* he says that he has always been
intrigued by "facts and people who give me the illusion of a dream." On
one occasion, at the beginning of the war, he spent several months deliberately provoking a rich and varied series of dreams by the food he ate, by
using drugs, and by his general way of life[3] (an incident transposed to
Marbre, where Ferréol Buq spends some time in the same activity).
More recently, he has experimented with a variety of drugs, and he says
in one interview: "I have taken hallucinogenic drugs, hashish, cocaine,
opium and various kinds of mushroom, LSD." The results seem to have
been disappointing, for he adds: "I prefer *directed reverie,* which leads
much further into the domain of the fantastic and the occult than any drug
can—at least for me."[4]

Mandiargues uses dreams in his work for the liberating and expanding effect that they have on the imagination. He also delights in
dreams because of what they reveal of the hidden depths of the human
psyche. Beside his frequently expressed longing to escape the tyranny of
self, there coexists a marked interest in the nature of the self, and especially in the recesses of the human personality that are revealed in
dreams. Freudian theory insists that much of our repressed instinct, our
darker self, is released in symbolic form in dreams, and this in itself is
enough to account for Mandiargues's interest in them.

In *Troisième Belvédère* he makes several comments on modern
artists that leave no doubt about his fascination with what lies at the
bottom of the human mind. He says that one of the reasons for his strong
attachment to modern art is that its creators have ceased exploring the
world of objects in order to examine "a certain necessity or fantasy inside
them." When writing of such artists as Alexandre Bonnier, Max Ernst,
Giorgio Morandi, and Giacometti in this volume, he comments particularly on the element of self examination in their works. He says, for

example, that Max Ernst's method is "like that of a psychiatrist exploring a disorganized consciousness." He argues in *Deuxième Belvédère* that Bosch fascinates us even today because of the symbolic representation of the unconscious in his paintings, and that the Fontainebleau School of painters is capable of arresting modern man's attention because it reveals "the marvels and the monsters that his unconscious hides." His view of the artist as examiner of his own self is perhaps best summed up by his definition of the painter in *Bona l'amour et la peinture* as "an eye (directed inwards as often as outwards)."

Mandiargues's views on literature show a similar preoccupation. He sees Nodier's work as an exploration of the dark corners of the mind, and he points out in *Troisième Belvédère* that "the role of the unconscious is sovereign in the inspiration and organization of *La Fée aux miettes*." Rousseau, that most introspective of all writers, is praised by him because: "His unease and the extremely penetrating look he casts over himself, his examination of 'erotic man' within himself, his curiosity for the first troubles of the child's soul, have not grown old in nearly two centuries."[5] The novel is, for Mandiargues, an important tool of self-analysis, and he claims in *Troisième Belvédère* that it is, above all, "the mirror of the novelist." Poetry too reveals the mysteries of the poet's self, and the title of one of Mandiargues's articles might sum up his view of the poet's role in this respect: "The poet paints his portrait when writing."[6]

Knowing Mandiargues's association with the surrealists, and his predilection for surrealist art, we should be surprised neither by his interest in dreams nor by his fascination with the unconscious. One of the goals of the surrealists was to reveal the depths of the self. They placed great emphasis on the role of the unconscious both in life and in art. In his *Les Dessous d'une vie ou la pyramide humaine*, Paul Eluard sees life as a pyramid, the tip of which is our waking self, and its broad base is the unconscious that supports and underlies it. Surrealists like him sought to release the unconscious by such techniques as automatic writing. This was supposed to remove artistic creation from the restraint of reason, and it bears an obvious resemblance to the special state of reverie or dreamlike trance that Mandiargues believes necessary when writing. (In fact, he says that the stories in *Le Musée noir* and *Soleil des loups* are the result of something akin to automatic writing.)[7]

These interests link Mandiargues not only to the surrealists, but to myth. The mythical hero's journey may be interpreted as a quest for the forces hidden in himself, and the deity whom he meets as the self that contains them. Myth recounts symbolically a journey inward, and one of its main functions is "to initiate the individual into the order of realities of his own psyche, guiding him toward his own spiritual enrichment and realization."[8] When the hero travels to the center of the universe, where the forces of life and death are to be found, he is also traveling to the center of his own being, where equally potent forces exist. "The passage of the mythological hero," writes Campbell, "may be overground, incidentally; fundamentally it is inward—into depths where obscure resistances are overcome, and long lost forgotten powers are revivified."[9] The gods, demons, and monsters that he meets on this journey are but the personification of the forces within him, "powers of the soul as well as of the living world."[10]

It is perfectly legitimate to see the mythical journey in Mandiargues's fiction as a journey into the self. We are encouraged in this interpretation by his explanation in *Le Désordre de la mémoire* of his goal in writing *Le Cadran lunaire:* "I sought through it to know myself better and to draw from darkness the hidden face of my deepest self." In *Troisième Belvédère* he has said that his object in writing fiction is: "To make a mirror for myself." He uses the same image in *Le Désordre de la mémoire* to explain that his characters represent aspects of himself, and that Conrad Mur, for example, is "another reflection of myself in a dark looking-glass." These comments go a long way toward explaining the presence of reflective surfaces in so many of his works, surfaces in which his characters observe themselves and discover hidden aspects of their nature. There are mirrors all over Jean de Lugio's room, in the room where Marceline's parents sleep, in front of Phébé Nova's bed, on the tomb in "Armoire de lune," on the bedroom walls in "Le Triangle ambigu." The knife blade in which the hero of "Peau et couteau" contemplates his image is also a mirror of the self, and the man's name is Salluste Tain—*tain* being the French word for the silvering on the back of a mirror.

Mandiargues's characters, like their creator, have an avid desire to see themselves, to observe themselves from the outside. Rebecca tries to imagine what she must seem like to her lover, and she frequently scrutinizes herself in the looking-glass. Vanina, lying unclothed on her bed, attempts to see herself through the eyes of the man watching her. The desire to leave their self and look at it from the outside is obviously linked to the longing to escape the bonds of selfhood that we have already discussed. It comes from deep within the human psyche, as Mandiargues makes clear when writing of Marie Mors, the heroine of "L'Etudiante" *(Soleil des loups)*. When she looks at her future, Marie is also contemplating herself from outside. Yet what she sees, while existing independently of her, seems to come from the depths of her mind. Mandiargues says: "Marie finds nothing that she does not already know, for it is her own image and the representation of the figures of her dreams that she discovers."

Besides the mirrors, there is another important image of self-discovery: the window. Windows abound in Mandiargues's stories, and they are symbolic openings onto the self. It is through a window that

Daniel first gains access to Rebecca's room, to Rebecca herself, and to the fulfillment of his desires. In *Le Lis de mer*, Vanina's future lover watches her through a window, and Vanina herself begins her journey toward the man who is the accomplishment of her deepest longings by leaving through "a window that opened onto the great wild night." Marceline Caïn leaves by a window when she goes to confront her darkest urges, and Damien in "Le Pont" reaches Camille de Hur through the window of her castle.

The glimpses of the self afforded by such means are not always pleasant. The journey into the dark regions of the mind is, like the mythical hero's quest, beset with difficulties and disagreeable surprises. The individual who undertakes this journey has to confront and accept the less pretty side of himself, the cruel, dangerous, and sadistic urges that lurk in all of us, and that Malraux has called man's "demons."[11] In *Troisième Belvédère* Mandiargues agrees with Baudelaire that there is a "latent Lucifer ensconced in every human heart." As an admirer of the Marquis de Sade, of the eroticism of such writers as Réage and Apollinaire, and as the author himself of a sado-erotic work, he is well away of this "Lucifer." He has expressed its dark presence in many of the cruel scenes that have already been mentioned in this study, has recognized it in his own self, and has admitted in *Le Désordre de la mémoire*: "In truth, I believe myself to be a sado-masochist."

But man is not all ugly and evil in Mandiargues's view. His vision of the duality of all things extends to man himself. He believes that we share the mixture of good and evil, light and dark, beautiful and ugly that may be observed in the surrounding world. The dual forces that constitute life also lie at the center of man's being. Whether the mythical quest is understood as being inward or outward, it leads to the discovery of the same twin forces.

In one article, Mandiargues regrets that evil, darkness, and cruel passions are part of human nature. Writing of the Hopi Indians, he expresses delight at their closeness to the natural world, but laments that evil as well as good comes of this. "It is distressing," he says, "to find confirmation of the presence of evil in the human heart, as it is to find it within nature."[12] More often, however, he accepts with equanimity the streak of evil within man. Part of the attraction that manichaeistic religions hold for him is that, as well as seeing a duality in the world, they see it as part of man's nature too. He inclines to this point of view himself, and writes in *Troisième Belvédère*: "The presence of evil alongside good within nature is obvious once one examines it from a 'moral' point of view, and the usefulness, if not the necessity of evil in the rhythm of existence in living beings and even in inanimate matter should strike any unprejudiced observer."

To pretend that the uglier side of human nature does not exist is abhorrent to Mandiargues. He prefers the attitude of such writers as Milton, Blake, Maturin, and Lautréamont, who openly depict "the dark underside of creation."[13] A writer like Joyce Mansour, who shows a keen interest in what many consider the "vicious" or "perverse" aspects of human behavior is merely showing her love of the world itself, for this "evil side of the universe" is as much part of creation as its more obviously beautiful one.[14]

Man's demons are frequently present in Mandiargues's work and are symbolized in a variety of ways. They are the monstrous creatures, the beasts that lurk behind all his characters, invisible yet ever-present. They are the huge fish that Conrad Mur imagines under the ice of the frozen lake, hiding just under the surface like man's ugly impulses beneath the level of consciousness. They are the marine creatures that his fiancée has seen hauled ashore, the thought of which, as he visualizes them just beneath his feet, makes Conrad's flesh crawl. Ferréol Buq too sees enormous, ugly fish drawn from the murky depths of a lake which may itself be taken as symbolic of the dark reaches of the unconscious. Vanina is acutely aware of the creatures at the bottom of the pools by the seashore and of the currents beneath the apparently placid and harmless sea, currents that could bear her away as easily as the urges beneath her own calm demeanor. She is horrified and fascinated by this possibility, and both these emotions are conveyed in the air of exquisitely frightened attention with which she listens to villagers' tales of beasts that lurk in the night and of giant fish that come ashore after dark. That she is tempted to toy with the demons that these monsters represent is obvious in the scene where she plays with an insect on the shore. With a kind of sadistic thrill, she catches several other insects and feeds them to the first one, watching intently as it devours them.

In classical psychoanalysis, suppressed urges often manifest themselves in dreams and visions of animals that embody the "bestial" nature of man. The large black pig and the bull that Vanina notices as she goes into the wood may, therefore, be seen as representations of these urges within her. A similar interpretation may be put on the huge stone pig's head that presides over the erotic excesses of the skaters in "L'Archéologue" (Soleil des loups), on the sheep in "Le Sang de l'agneau" (Le Musée noir) which seem to share Marceline's confused emotions as she is raped, and on the dog in "Adive" (Mascarets) which is the direct cause of the heroine's sexual pleasure.[15] In a short story called "Rodogune," from Feu de braise, the main character is accompanied all the time by a pet ram, which may also be taken as the "animal" side of her that follows her everywhere.

If we interpret myth as being a journey inward, the wilderness that the hero must cross in his quest may be seen as the unpleasant, dangerous reaches of the self. Anyone who delves into himself must cross this unsavory territory, as Vanina must cross an area of sewage, Captain Idalium pick his way through junk and driftwood, Sigismond tread the dingy streets of Barcelona, and Ferréol face a dark forest. Society normally tolerates few of the monsters and demons encountered in such places, which is why, in Mandiargues's stories, these areas are patrolled by forces representing social restraint. Vanina has to elude the carabinieri who would prevent her entering the wood, and Rebecca has to be careful of police, speed limits, and similar restraints placed on the instinctual urges represented by her motorcycle. In "Mil neuf cent trente-trois," a story in *Sous la lame*, Abel Foligno, disturbed by violent impulses, finds himself outside a prison guarded by a group of policemen and is suddenly reminded that he must control the passions raging inside him.

In both Freudian theory and Mandiargues's imagination, the demons that beset man are nearly always sexual. In fact, it is in sexual activity that man, according to Mandiargues, reveals himself most clearly. Exploring the erotic is, therefore, one way of exploring the very basis of man's behavior, and he says in *Le Désordre de la mémoire* that "it seems to me that sex reveals man and woman." Rebecca and Vanina do not fully discover what lies within them (although they have intimations of it) until they meet the men who release their true nature. The hero of "L'Enfantillage," from *Feu de braise*, as he has sexual relations with a prostitute, travels back in time to his childhood, reliving the origins of his self and the incidents that made him what he is. In "Miranda", one of the pieces in *Sous la lame*, the point is made in a rather startling fashion. This is the story of a brutal frontier guard who stops a passing girl, takes her to his hut and attempts to rape her.[16] As he embraces her, he sees himself reflected in her eyes in all his ugly lust. Then, suddenly, she is transformed into his double, and he is embracing himself, face to face with his own sexual desire.

Of these sexual drives, one of the most potent, and one which the individual often finds difficult to accept, is the incestuous urge. Mandiargues is avidly interested in this aspect of man's psychology, and has admitted that "incestuous love is a form of excessive love that seems fascinating to me."[17] The erotic passion that Isabella Morra's brothers show in torturing her is one example of how this theme finds its way into his work. Another one is "Le Théâtre de Pornopapas" from *Porte dévergondée* in which a man, after traveling through dingy and dirty streets that represent his darker nature, comes to a theater where he contemplates his own deepest impulses in the form of an actor called Oedipos, who exhibits a large artificial phallus while singing "It's for my mother."[18]

The incestuous instinct may take the form of a desire to return to the womb, and the watery depths into which some of Mandiargues's characters descend are obvious symbols of the womb. The side street in "Le passage Pommeraye" *(Le Musée noir),* with its glaucous light, is compared to an aquarium and a well while Conrad Mur does descend into the very sea (the French word for which is pronounced in the same way as the word for *mother).* The spirals and mazes that we have noted in several stories symbolize the internal organs of the female and access to the womb.[19] The goddess herself, the goal of the hero's quest, is the great mother, and the character who achieves union with her is also achieving incestuous return to the womb of mother nature.

In *Le Musée noir* there is one story which is a particularly good illustration of this theme. "L'Homme du parc Monceau" is Mandiargues's most sustained allegory of incestuous sexual intercourse. This is an unusual story (even for Mandiargues), all the more striking because the strange events it describes are set in a familiar place in a well-known city and against a background of recognizable details. It contains many of his usual fictional elements: a character who changes shape, a moonlit night, a temple-cum-tomb, ritual cleansing, an atmosphere of extraordinary events about to happen, and a whole series of sexual allusions and symbols. It opens with a man taking off his clothes in the deserted street on a moonlit night and then flattening himself into a serpentine shape and sliding under the railings of the parc Monceau. He enters the Etruscan tomb in the park, in order, we are told, to celebrate his marriage to "the Great Cat Mammon." *(Mammon,* incidentally, is pronounced rather like *maman.)* After he has been washed and perfumed by a pair of ugly old women, he enters a corridor where the roof is supported by columns kept rigid by the caresses of a group of beautiful girls. The Great Cat Mammon lies at the center of the tomb, like the deity in an inner sanctum. It is womb-like in its warmth and protectiveness, "a purring and warm mountain." The man approaches it, and is absorbed in "the depths of a sea of fur." *(Sea* in French, it should be noted again, is pronounced the same way as *mother.)*

Although the man in this story seems only too willing to abandon himself to his incestuous urges, the deep-seated impulses in man can be dangerous. When Marceline Caïn gives in to her darker side, she commits murder; Captain Idalium's cruel nature, as represented by the animals in the cave, kills him. Two pieces of fiction in particular may be read as warnings of the awesome powers hidden in man's psyche.

One of these, "Le Tombeau d'Aubrey Beardsley," is also from *Le Musée noir.* In this tale, man's demons are represented by the Negro actor Gabalus, who performs at the Great Dreamhall in Memphis—aptly named, since it is in dreams that many such instinctual urges are freed. His performance of Othello (who incarnates the demons of sexual jealousy) so stirs up the frenzy of the women in the audience that, for days afterwards, they rampage in the throes of "a furious desire for black flesh," while the men are possessed by intense jealousy and vent their rage on the black population. Gabalus is forced to hide in an obscure corner of the town, accessible only through a particularly decayed and filthy district.

The incident of Gabalus forms a kind of overture, introducing the theme and putting the reader in the frame of mind to appreciate the rest of the story. In this part, the narrator goes to a party given by a group of female giants. On entering the house, he is made to eat a disgusting concoction of eggs cooked on the head of a statue representing a dog. This "ceremony of humiliation" is a kind of initiation rite by which he accepts the uglier side of himself. All the other men at the party are dwarfs, indicating by their stature how puny men are beside their sexual desires, represented by the women. There follows a "capilliary dinner" served by naked women in wigs, during which hair napkins are used and such curious dishes as "perruques surprises," "langue de boeuf farcie de cheveux à la moutarde," and "chevelures confites" are served. Since hair is frequently a sexual fetish, these continual references to it reinforce the erotic undertones of the meal.

After they have eaten, one of the women, who has taken a particular interest in the narrator, leads him to an alcove where the decor represents a variety of sado-erotic scenes. Although tempted by the beautiful giant, he takes no liberties with her, for, like the urges she symbolizes, she is very powerful. The other men are not so careful, and quarrel with the women. In the ensuing battle, they are easily overcome by the giants.

The second of the tales which warn of the dangers of man's demons is from *Soleil des loups*. This story, entitled with grisly humor "La Vision capitale," is worthy of Poe at his blackest. Its heroine, Hester Algernon, suffers because she toys unwisely with forces inside her that prove, in the end, to be beyond her control. She is preoccupied by the ease with which the veneer of civilization may be stripped away to reveal the beast in us, and one of her hobbies conveys symbolically this interest: she tries, by careful breeding, to produce wolves from domestic dogs. When invited to a fancy dress ball, she chooses to go as an animal—in this case, a rooster. The donning of her costume is not just a disguise, but a yielding to her true self, and she describes it as "no caricature, but a veritable state of possession." Unfortunately, when she arrives at the château where the ball is to be given, she discovers that she has arrived several days too early. The concierge (who is, on one level, her superego, and on another the threshold guardian of myth), allows her in only after questioning her at length.

The atmosphere now becomes fraught with anticipation and fear.

Hester is given a room for the night, but feels ill at ease in it. She notices, with growing apprehension, that the decor represents various scenes of bloody battles and monstrous animals, while the furniture is carved to resemble contorted limbs. She manages to go to sleep, but is awakened to find that the demons she once took so lightly are in the room with her. She sees a naked man, filthy in appearance, capering around in the red light of the dying fire. In his hands he holds an old woman's blood-splattered head, and, like someone plucking a chicken, he is tearing out handfuls of its hair and throwing them in the fire, where they flare and crackle. When Hester screams, he glances at her, then leaps out the window, grasping the head by its hair.

Hester persuades herself that this was a dream, but, next morning, she learns that a madman has escaped from an asylum and decapitated a woman. This discovery—the revelation of what lies buried in every human heart—deranges her mind, and she reverts to an animal state. She now wanders the woods, half crazed, keeping by preference to its darkest, most decayed regions.

These warnings that we should not toy with the explosive power of the forces within us are counterbalanced by the advice that we should not ignore them either. Conrad Mur in "L'Archéologue" stands as an example of where this can lead. His dry, dusty life, his fear of women, his neurotic awareness of the monsters below the surface of his being are all indications of his refusal to accept his sexual nature. He is attracted to Bettina only because she is cold and rather sexless, and he abandons her when she begins to resemble other women. Then he has the temerity to reject the goddess herself, the representative of sexuality, life, and the "bestial" in man. Her destruction of him shows that we must accept this side of ourselves, for ignoring it does not render it harmless.

The sensible attitude is to accept our dual nature. Two of Mandiargues's other pieces of short fiction, both to be found in Sous la lame, point out that man is a strange mixture of good and evil, innocence and crime, and that all these sides of his nature must be taken into account. "Peau et couteau" is a brief, uncomplicated parable. It opens with the hero, Salluste Tain, looking at his reflection in the blade of a knife—an instrument of violence that reflects him in more ways than one. The image is split in two by the shape of the blade, symbolizing the division in Salluste himself. His mind travels back to an incident that happened a few hours previously in a hotel room. He was embracing a woman when her hand happened upon a knife left in an open drawer. Jestingly, he had taken it and placed it at her breast. Then, giving in to an impulse, he stabbed her. He now realizes that this murderous urge was as much a part of him as his usual inoffensive nature.

"Mil neuf cent trente-trois" is a rather more complex story

founded on the play of opposites, and it is presided over by the ambiguous presence of the planet Venus. Its hero, Abel Foligno, is tormented by troubling urges, by demons whose presence he sees in several cruel and lascivious images in the world around him: the evil-smelling bats he imagines hanging in dark archways, the phallic shaped stone on which he rests while wandering in Ferrara, the monster tearing a human prey that he sees on the cathedral façade. Even the verse by Tennyson that he quotes to his wife has hints of blackness and evil in it: "Come into the garden, Maud/For the black bat, night, has flown." His wife, whose name really is Maud, seems a rather prim person who disapproves of his occasional bursts of ribaldry. She is especially shocked when he makes up a story about Tennyson's sexual relations with Queen Victoria. Both Tennyson and Victoria are the very essence of respectability, and it says much about her character that she reveres them.

One night, Abel is almost overcome by the desire to batter his sleeping wife's head in. Horrified, he rushes into the street, trying to understand "the enemy who had taken up residence in his meninges." He looks up and sees the evening star, symbol of all that is dual and ambiguous. Then he sees an open window, but he represses the urge to climb through it, for he is not yet ready to accept what might lie on the other side of this opening into the self. He decides, instead, to abandon his wife and the respectability that she represents, and he flees to Ferrara, "that most ambiguous of cities, cradle of Savonarola and tomb of Lucrezia Borgia, asylum of Tasso in his madness, favorite stopping place of Carlo Gesualdo, Prince of Venosa, famous murderer and sublime musician." His demons come to the fore again: he dresses negligently and takes to frequenting the prostitutes' quarter. The atmosphere of the city is particularly favorable to the instincts of violence since the local fascists are in the midst of a celebration, and a heady brutality emanates from the black-shirted revelers. Finally, Abel enters a brothel, where a prostitute wearing an artificial phallus offers to whip him. Although he refuses at first, he later accepts her offer and becomes, as his biblical name suggests he should, her victim. The story ends on an air of dark apprehension, but Abel has at least come to terms with the duality of his nature, as symbolized by the hermaphrodite disguise of the prostitute, and he has abandoned the pretence of purity represented by his wife.

Both this prostitute and the figure whom Conrad Mur meets are the goddess who lies at the end of the hero's journey. The lesson of myth, interpreted on a psychological level, is that she also lies at the heart of every individual, and to achieve harmony within us, we must recognize her presence. According to Jung, all individuals have in their unconscious a female element that he calls the *anima*. It is this aspect of our psyche that produces our archetypal image of woman (incarnated in the goddess of myth): she is a mother figure, connected with the earth or with water, can be "two-sided, or has two aspects, a light and a dark," and is often an alluring siren.[20] In Mandiargues's work, she can also be threatening and inimical to the male. Conrad Mur associates women with death and decay, and the goddess does indeed destroy him in the end. In "Le Tombeau d'Aubrey Beardsley," the giant women are also hostile to the men, and turn upon them. Even "L'Homme du parc Monceau" may be seen as depicting women and the female principle in this light, and the whole story can be interpreted as an allegory of a sexual fiasco produced by a devouring, castrating female force. The hero is a flabby, rubbery character, and the difficulty of achieving erection is hinted at by the efforts to which the maidens have to go in order to keep the columns supporting the roof rigid. The man is literally devoured by the womb-like cat, and, at that moment, the tomb collapses, presumably because the columns are no longer erect.

To pursue this Jungian line of thought, there is also an *animus* or male side of every being. The women in Mandiargues's fiction who discover the solar deity are encountering this principle in themselves. It too can be inimical, especially when linked to a hostile, destructive father figure. Such a figure appears in *La Marge*, where the image of Sigismond's father accompanies him, seeming to do battle with his memory of his wife and to come between him and his love for her. But, at the end of the novel, these two images are reconciled, and Sigismond achieves harmony. When they discover the deity in its hermaphrodite form, Mandiargues's heroes and heroines accept the dual nature of their selves, achieve the combination of *animus* and *anima* that is necessary for psychic harmony.

In the psychology of Jung, great emphasis is placed on the need for this harmony with the self, and recognition of both the *animus* and the *anima* is essential for this to happen. To reach down to the self and harmonize its different parts "necessitates acceptance of what is inferior in one's nature, as well as what is irrational and chaotic."[21] This process of becoming aware of all that is in the self is called "individuation" by Jung, and Mandiargues's characters, in their journey to the center of the self, are going through the toils of individuation. They discover the ugly and "inferior" parts of their personality, and for those who accept them, there is a sense of harmony. One might compare this process to the flowers that Vanina sees growing on the seashore. These beautifully formed and fragrant objects grow in decay and sewage, just as the beauty of self-acceptance grows on recognition of all that is ugly in the self.

The mandalas and geometric shapes so common in Mandiargues's writings also have a role to play in the acceptance of the self. Jung has pointed out that mandala symbolism often occurs in dreams, and that it expresses the desire for harmony that comes from recognition of the true self. The center of the mandala represents the center of the self, the place where we must travel in the individuation process. Hence, when Sarah Mose finds herself inside the geometrically cut diamond, when the characters of "Le Marronnier" *(Mascarets)* sit inside the circles and squares of the garden, when Rebecca imagines herself in a ruby, they have come symbolically to knowledge of the self. The case of Ferréol Buq illustrates the harmony and sense of peace that such knowledge produces. The statue that he discovers is set at the center of a mandala, so, when he goes inside it, he is entering the self. Its hermaphrodite nature indicates the *anima/animus* duality of the psyche, and, by entering it through its sexual parts, he is symbolically recognizing his own sexual nature. He then goes past the paintings representing his inner demons and comes to the head where he achieves the harmony that results from recognition of the self.

The unity of all things that Ferréol grasps at this moment is in the night and the surrounding countryside, but it is in himself too. He comes to knowledge of the Platonic harmony of the spheres that is suggested by the title of this section of the novel: "The Platonic Bodies." His self is part of that unity, and Jungian psychology again helps us understand why. For Jung, the self consists of "the awareness on the one hand of our unique natures, and on the other of our intimate relationship with all life, not only human but animal and plant, and even that of inorganic matter and the cosmos itself."[22] Discovery of the self leads, as in moments of "panic" communion, to the realization that our nature participates in the whole of life.

The self and the world are one because the "panic" forces in nature are also inside man, and this is why man shares the duality of the outside world. One of the lessons of myth is that the divine forces, the godhead, are within as well as without. It teaches that "the essence of oneself and the essence of the world . . . are one."[23] Mandiargues's heroes discover that the divine is inside the individual. As Jung has said: "Myth is the revelation of the divine life in man."[24] Campbell puts it this way: "The two—the hero and his ultimate goal, the seeker and the found—are thus understood as the outside and the inside of a single self-mirrored mystery, which is identical with the mystery of the manifest world."[25] Mandiargues does not talk of divine powers, the godhead, or the divinity within us in exactly these terms, but he shares the point of view that man partakes of the life forces around him. To use his own words: "The microcosm of the human mind is in the image of the universal macrocosm."[26]

8

Realism and Fantasy

Ce qu'il y a d'admirable dans le fantastique, c'est qu'il n'y a plus de
fantastique, il n'y a plus que le réel.
André Breton, *Premier Manifeste du Surréalisme*

MANDIARGUES CREATES A WORLD OF FANTASY where the unexpected, the unusual, and the impossible become the norm, yet one very striking aspect of this fantasy is its realism of detail. His is a world unknown outside of the pages of his works, but it remains a peculiarly real and familiar world. Critics have not been slow to point this out, and comments on his "magic realism," his "minute realism in the unreal," his "specialized technician's vocabulary," and descriptions of him as "a realist of the imaginary" are typical.[1] Mandiargues has himself insisted that "in order to achieve an atmosphere of dream or reverie, the most minute realism is essential."[2] He claims that "one can only succeed in making a very exaggerated scene real, or at least alive, by minute realism," and he quotes the surrealists, and particularly Aragon, as examples of how this can be done.[3]

Among the many instances that one might mention of Mandiargues's realistic fantasy is his description in *Soleil des loups* of a group of enormous insects. The narrator of "Le Pain rouge," when he shrinks in size and enters a hole in a piece of bread, encounters insects which, because he is now so tiny, seem monstrously large. Rendered fantastic and unreal by their size, they are nevertheless depicted in realistic detail: "Their bodies, with their arched backs and flat stomachs, although reminiscent of the heavy forms of the tortoise's shell, were muffled in a thick fleece that seemed to have come directly from a dyeing vat, for nature, when it comes to clothing animals, is not usually so generous with the fine light tyrian crimson that marvelously colored the dress of these creatures. Six legs jutted from the fur, small in proportion to the bulk that they bore, jointed, shiny, as hard as if the sections of which they were made had been molded in mahogany-colored plastic; and they terminated in hooks and saw-teeth perfectly adapted to gripping the terrain at any angle."

The sense of curiosity that is so essential a part of Mandiargues's nature, his inquiring attitude toward the world around him, his love of natural beauty, and of interesting objects all play a role in his attention to detail. He is avidly interested in everything that he encounters, and he says that, when he is walking in the countryside, he stops continually to turn over stones, to remove loose tree bark, so that he may observe the insects beneath them, the unexpected life that is hidden from view.[4] Naturally enough, when he contributed a regular article to the *Nouvelle Revue Française*, the series was called "Curiosity of the Month." In fact, he has described curiosity as "one of man's essential virtues, worthy of being added to the three theological and the four cardinal virtues."[5] In his own case, this searching gaze turned on the world easily becomes outright avidity, an almost physical desire to possess the world.

This all makes Mandiargues a passionate observer of details. One critic has spoken of his "taste and obsession for the minute,"[6] and "obsession" is certainly not too strong a word. Mandiargues has agreed that love of detail is a part of his work, and has pointed out that he has some very respectable predecessors in this respect: Balzac, Dickens, and the Russian novelists, among others.[7] In *Le Désordre de la mémoire*, he attributes his delight in minute observation partly to the fact that he is short-sighted and has to look very carefully at objects in order to see them properly.

There are innumerable passages of his writing where the atmosphere of magic and fantasy is based directly on observation of minutiae. One example of this is the street in "Le passage Pommeraye." We are shown, with deliberate concern for every speck of dust and physical characteristic, the shop windows, their peculiar contents, the gallery of statues, the glass roof. Yet the whole place breathes an air of menace, as though the fabric of the real is about to be rent by some unimaginable event. Another scene based on meticulous observation is the one in which Pascal Bénin splits open the stone, and we see the three tiny creatures emerge, every facial feature and every strand of their flowing hair clearly visible. The stone from which they come is displayed to us with a geologist's care for accuracy of vocabulary and description. Similar scenes abound, and it would be pointless to enumerate them here—the reader may find them for himself by opening any volume of Mandiargues's writing. Of all modern writers, he is one of the most visual, one of those who makes us *see* this world.

Many of the places that serve as the locale for his work do actually exist, and may easily be recognized. There really is a passage Pommeraye in Nantes, but its air of mystery is contributed by the writer. The Barrio Chino in Barcelona also exists, as do the towns that Rebecca crosses on her motorcycle. In "Adive" from *Mascarets*, the boulevard Saint-Germain between the rue de Rennes and the carrefour Danton is clearly and recognizably described, but it serves as a starting point for a tale of dark adventure and strange forces at work. The parc Monceau is as Mandiargues depicts it, but he has invested it with a sense of foreboding that the casual visitor does not usually notice in the real park. In all these cases, he has anchored tales of the extraordinary and the unknown to real places that many readers will recognize.

Even those parts of his work that are purely imaginary still remain firmly tied to the real world. Dreams and the many oneiric sequences in his fiction have everyday reality, the waking world, as their point of departure. The vision of the naked girl among the coffins is, we learn at the end of the story, provoked by memories of the narrator's visit to the prostitutes' quarter of the town. It ends as the woman refers to an ambulance siren, and the sleeper awakes to hear a siren in the street outside. In "L'Isis du Colisée" from Le Cadran lunaire, Mandiargues recounts a dream in which he discovers a statue of a naked swimmer. On awakening, he realizes that it was caused by memories of a nightclub called the Coliséum, where, in 1933 or 1934, he had seen girls swimming in a large illuminated tank. This had become mingled with memories of a statue that he had been shown in Rome, and the result of these real events was a dream of haunting, unreal beauty.

Mandiargues has studied and experimented enough with dreams to know that the more they are tied to the world around us, the more vivid they are. He knows that, although time has no meaning in them, they are nevertheless linked to a world governed by time. He is aware, for instance, that the dreams he deliberately provoked while living in Monaco were the product of a particular time when events in the outside world drove him to make these experiments. His desire to escape the tyranny of an oppressive time and disastrous events was the catalyst for his oneiric experiences. Consequently, these dreams were marked by the times, and "reflected more or less . . . the color of the age."[8]

So wedded to the world around him is his world of fantasy that he documents himself extensively on the places, events, and objects that he depicts. Before writing La Motocyclette, he drove five times over the route that Rebecca takes, and he rode a Harley-Davidson machine like hers in order to know what it was like.[9] The wealth of detail concerning the functioning of motorcycles and the use of the correct technical vocabulary show that he also documented himself carefully on the subject. La Marge shows equally careful preparation of the ground, and Mandiargues explains in Le Désordre de la mémoire that many of the scenes and events that Sigismond observes in the streets of Barcelona are based on ones that the writer himself noted while walking there.

Mandiargues has said: "I note the minutest details of the scenes which I am describing or the place where the action occurs. Like the naturalists, Flaubert in particular, I always visit the site which I plan to describe in my novel. With paper and pencil in hand, I jot down all the details and in a meticulous manner."[10] Rather than of Flaubert, one thinks of Zola, who rode on the footplate of a locomotive, making notes, before transforming the reality he observed into the grandiose epic of *La Bête humaine*. No attentive reader of Zola should be surprised by this comparison. Mandiargues's ideas and techniques are closely related to those of the surrealists, and, as J. H. Matthews has shown, although the themes and premises of the naturalists and the surrealists are very different, their vision and their effects are not so far apart.[11] Zola too is capable, although depicting things "realistically," of producing scenes of sheer surrealistic fantasy, as when he describes the disparate collection of objects sold in Mouret's store in *Au Bonheur des dames,* or when he infuses life into inanimate objects like the mine in *Germinal.* Mandiargues seems to be making much the same point when he says: "And I, by the way, see no antagonism between realism and surrealism. The first books of the surrealists, some of them, anyway, pushed realism further than was usual at the time."[12]

At the beginning of *Marbre,* we are given a glimpse of the creative process that turns objects of the world around the writer into the skeleton on which the flesh of fantasy is placed. In the first few pages, Mandiargues describes himself sitting at his desk, on which stand a paperweight and a list of girls' names. Then he notices an insect of the kind called *longicorne* in French, but whose German name, translated into French, would be *scarabée-bouc* ("goat-beetle") or *porc-volant* ("flying pig"). This provides him with the name of his hero—Ferréol Buq (from *bouc*)—and suggests that he is something of a "pig" by nature. The word *bouc* ("goat") also suggests sexual proclivities, and the list of girls' names on the desk combines with this idea to provide the hero's main characteristic: he is a sexual adventurer. The shape of the paperweight suggests the geometric stones around the statue that Ferréol discovers, and it provides the inspiration for one of the most critical incidents of the novel. Since the insect also reminds him of a woodpile crawling with similar insects, which he once saw in Italy, he decides to set the novel in that country. And it is thus that his imagination, dependent on the everyday world for its inspiration, weaves a web of fantasy and unlikely happenings.

By observing closely and allowing his creative genius to work on them, Mandiargues discovers in the world of banal objects and commonplace events hidden possibilities which lie latent there, waiting to be released. There are, in an insect, a paperweight, the objects in a shop window, the machinery of a motorcycle, a mysterious and compelling beauty, a power to fascinate and delight. One simply has to know how to look at things in order to see what Mandiargues, using typically surrealist terminology, calls the "marvelous." For him, the impulse to write, to create any work of art, comes from the feeling of marvel that the artist senses when looking at the world. He says that the most unexpected, the most banal, the most ordinary object may hold this magic. "Marvelous objects,"he writes in *Deuxième Belvédère*, "are innumerable in the outside world, from woman to poetry, from serpents to paintings, from the orchid to a wall in the suburbs, from wood burned or washed by the waves to a glacier, a pebble and a reef at low tide, from rock crystal to volcanoes, the praying mantis and the dusty assassin bug (not forgetting the dust itself)."

The world of everyday objects holds surprises for whoever looks at it attentively. (Pierre Mabille points out that the word "marvel" is etymologically linked to the idea of "things susceptible to or worthy of being looked at.")[13] Mandiargues says: "When one looks at the real world with great attention, when one fixes one's gaze on reality, well! reality is transformed into a kind of marvelous dream."[14] The painter Gnoli, he points out in *Troisième Belvédère*, "is passionately attentive to the most ordinary things that constitute the decor of man's life." From these things he creates works of poetic magic which show that awareness of the real world does not "exclude the rather special poetry that inhabits the most banal reality once it is viewed from a certain point of view."

Mandiargues's goal too is to make us see the world "from a certain point of view." As he explains in the preface to *Le Musée noir*, there are times when the world suddenly, unexpectedly, reveals its hidden secrets, provided that we know how to look at it. "The panorama set up by the senses in the human consciousness is not a very solid wall," he writes. "Pierced at every moment by holes, shaken by whirlwinds, it only blinds those who seek precisely nothing beyond its mediocre ready made." The cliffs of Berneval, for example, are more than mere white chalk. If one looks at them carefully, and in the right frame of mind, their color varies, one sees the effect of wind and water on them, one notices strange shapes in them, and they assume a new appearance altogether. The same may be said of many objects and materials: "coal, sand, soot, plaster, ice, snow, wool, gold, iron, lead, wood, moss, blood, bread, milk, wine."

In *Sous la lame*, Mandiargues writes of some bats hanging in a dark archway. His description of these creatures, as they are imagined by the hero of "Mil neuf cent trente-trois," shows exactly how banal or even unpleasant objects may reveal a strange attraction, and suggest peculiar images to the mind. He imagines the bats which "must have come back to the places where they hang when they sleep, taking on the forms of dried fruit, dirty little velvet sacks, severed and shriveled hands, discarded gloves, old purses, the wrinkled testicles of some pachyderm." In other passages, the graffiti on a statue, an insect discovered in a book, wild flowers growing on the seashore are picked out from the world of objects and displayed as a source of amazement.[15] Even the Paris Métro, in *Troisième Belvédère*, becomes an occasion of sheer delight, although for many people it is merely part of a deadening daily routine. Mandiargues is in the tradition of da Vinci, who, he points out in one article, advised aspiring artists to observe closely a stain on a wall, and to use it as a model to create works of art.[16] He is doing the same thing as Chirico, Roussel, and Cingria, who, he says in *Le Belvédère*, show us "the mystery of the everyday."

The revelation of the world in a new light may be compared to a process that Mandiargues describes in one of the prose poems in *L'Age de craie*. He says in "L'Œuf dans le paysage" that, if one looks through a blemish in glass, the world on the other side takes on different appearances depending on where one stands. Or is it, he asks, that the world has all these appearances anyway, and that the bubble in the glass merely enables us to see what is already there? This is a perfect image of Mandiargues's art, which gives us a new vision of the world in which we live by showing us what is already in it.

Mandiargues does exactly what the surrealists wanted to do: he reveals the latent content of objects by showing them in a new light. His technique for doing this is frequently the same as the surrealists' too: he puts together objects or events not usually associated, and creates new resonances between them. Three fairy figures dance beside a common stone; a kind of wardrobe stands in a graveyard; a huge hermaphrodite statue rises in a clearing in the woods. In one article, "Les Chefs-d'œuvre aux terrains vagues" from *Le Belvédère*, he describes Bernini's statue of Louis XIV, exiled to an unexpected and neglected corner of Versailles, where it interacts with its surroundings, and we suddenly see new possibilities in the statue. These aspects were already there, but remained latent until set beside things we do not normally associate with this work of art. This is strongly reminiscent of Magritte, who, in his paintings, fills a realistically drawn living room with enormous combs, matches, pin cushions, and shaving brushes, and, by so doing, creates strange relationships between them and makes us see them differently.[17]

In one of his few adverse comments, made in *Le Belvédère*, Mandiargues criticises the cubists for filling their paintings with objects without showing us anything new in them. Max Ernst, on the other hand, teaches us to see things anew. Merely to display the world around us is not enough; the artist must, like Ernst, reveal its latent possibilities. Writing in *Troisième Belvédère*, he says that the true artist is a *voyant*, someone gifted with the ability to see the underside of reality and to enable others to see it. He must be, like Chirico, a "great seer" or, like Svanberg, "an inspired individual who inspires." When we have experienced the kind of art of which Mandiargues is thinking, our very vision of reality is changed. When, for example, we read the poetry of Francis Ponge, we enter what he describes in *Le Cadran lunaire* as a world "where nothing is like what we once knew." Artists are magicians who transform the world for us, and the opinion that Mandiargues expresses of painters in *Troisième Belvédère* holds true for all artists: "The attitude of the painter is, then, promethean; his actions belong to magic categories rather than religious ones."

There is, in this comment, an implied warning against seeing a religious role for the artist: Mandiargues does not seek, in art, an escape from this world into a supernatural sphere. He does not turn his back on this world, but tries to reveal what is already in it. He makes this very clear in *Troisième Belvédère* when speaking of the Mexican artist Toledo: "What we are dealing with, I repeat, is akin to a mystic process, which is in the order of profound clairvoyance. Toledo's fantastic universe is not supernatural, it is part of nature transfigured, of nature stripped of the false mask that men have, in their cowardly way, put on it in order not to be bothered in their everyday occupations, it is part of nature refound." Only in this sense, of going beyond appearances to a deeper reality, is Mandiargues's idea of art a mystical one. It is Toledo's power to reveal what is already there that makes him "like a priest, a monk, or a sorcerer of forms." It is only because some artists have the ability to transport and delight us by their representations of *this world* that he calls them in *Le Désordre de la mémoire* "the most sacred priests." All of Mandiargues's conception of art is based on a recognition of this world, of its material reality, and its obsessive, weighty presence. The only transcendence that he seeks is the "transcendent materialism" that he sees in Francis Ponge's attention to detail *(Le Cadran lunaire)* or the "magic realism" of Flaubert *(Le Désordre de la mémoire)*.

The artist is also a "priest" or a "mystic" in that he is the instrument of mysterious forces. Mandiargues, like the surrealists, seems to believe that the writer and the painter are mediums through which the hidden beauty of the universe flows. In *Troisième Belvédère* he says that, when a writer like Breton is inspired by great themes, such as woman or love, he becomes "a kind of medium, and how violently he reacts in his choice and grouping of words when he is inhabited or visited by the greatest themes!" Mandiargues himself believes that he writes best when inspired this way. "I have always sought to write like someone obsessed, to write only in a state of obsession," he says in *Le Désordre de la mémoire*. Even more explicitly, he admits: "To give birth to a story, to a poem, something which I do not carry out easily and of whose success I

am never certain, I have to be in that special state that corresponds
somewhat, I would hope, to the sorcerer's trance in the ceremonies of
primitive peoples." The resemblance to the automatic writing practiced
by the surrealists is striking.

One might compare this conception of the artist (and, indeed, we
are almost invited to do so by Mandiargues's reference to sorcerers among
primitive peoples) to the role of the shaman in certain societies.[18] The
shaman is a kind of magician who, like the artist, sees and experiences
things which the rest of his people do not. These experiences come to him
when he is in a trance, and he then has to make them intelligible to
others. What is particularly interesting is that the shaman is also associated with myth. He is the guardian of traditional wisdom, enshrined
in myths, which he recites to his people when under the influence of
unseen powers. Shamans are, in Mircea Eliade's words, "the specialists of
trances, familiars of fantastic worlds, who nourish, increase and elaborate
traditional mythological motifs."[19]

Mandiargues too believes that there are unseen forces around us.
As we saw in chapter 3, he argues that they are latent in the world itself,
and that the artist is especially sensitive to their presence. Many artists
see signs, messages, and omens, like the ones that set Rebecca off on her
mythical quest. Unica Zürn, for example, has "a passion for deciphering
signs," and Leonora Carrington is able to look at objects and events and
see meanings to which others are blind.[20] Mandiargues's wife Bona has
often shown this artist's hypersensitivity to strange forces, and in *Le
Désordre de la mémoire* he tells how, in many of her paintings, and for
some reason unknown to her, she depicted a small, lonely child. Years
later, after the birth of their daughter, they realized that their own child
had the same features as the girl in the painting. As an example of his own
sensitivity to such forces, there is an incident, described in the same
volume, that took place on the day that he learned of Benjamin Péret's
death. He was in Venice at the time, thinking sadly of his old friend,
when he saw a calf's head floating under the Bridge of Sighs, and it
seemed to him that a Péret poem had taken concrete form before his
eyes. It was as though Péret was addressing a sign to him. Both events are
akin to what the surrealists called "objective chance"—strange, inexplicable coincidences that they took as signs that, beyond appearances, there
were unseen forces at work.

As we know, such signs appear frequently in Mandiargues's
books, and we have mentioned several of them that set his heroes and
heroines off on their quest. There are, in addition to these initial signs,
many others, for his characters live in a world that continually tries to
communicate with them. Conrad Mur, in "L'Archéologue" (*Soleil des
loups*) is typical of them, for he "believes in premonitions and signs

scarcely less than one of those ancient Etruscans or Romans who are his companions day and night." Consequently, as he watches the sea rise and fall, he knows instinctively that it is beckoning him, and, when he realizes that Bettina is wearing a black scarf he knows that disaster awaits him. The hero of *La Marge,* on the other hand, although he receives many such signs, does not recognize them. As he leaves his room to go to the post office, he suddenly remembers how his wife sits in front of her dressing table mirror, turns it slowly away, and says: "Adieu, Sergine Montefiore." In the street, an old woman selling lottery tickets cries, "para hoy," meaning that the draw for prizes is that day, but also a sign that the day will bring Sigismond bad news. He passes near a bridge that reminds him of the Bridge of Sighs, and, on the post office he sees a coat of arms surmounted by a bat, which, he realizes, is "an animal of evil omen." Later in the novel, he receives many signs that his own death is approaching, as does Rebecca when she draws near to the point where she will die. A glance at almost any story by Mandiargues will reveal many more such signs.[21]

Mandiargues's world, like Baudelaire's, speaks to the attentive listener—through familiar objects, tiny details, dreams, omens, and signs. This world provokes a deep sense of marvel, of delight and even of passion in Mandiargues by its capacity to reveal unsuspected depths, and he creates his books in order to make us share the same feelings. Art is, in his opinion, a product of the artists' emotion. When a writer or a painter or a sculptor creates a work of art, "it is a matter of finding what moved us in an animal, plant or pebble (or in the appearance of water, air or fire) and giving birth to an object (paintings and statues are as much objects as poems) which is capable of producing similar emotion in others."[22] Those like Audiberti, who live "in an immense and perpetual astonishment," Eluard, who expresses "the bewildering marvel of life," and Rousseau, who "wrote only when uplifted by emotion and to communicate his emotion," are Mandiargues's ideal artists.[23] He has tried to emulate them, and he claims that "I write under the influence of emotion; I write also to try and rediscover my emotion."[24]

Strangely, these vibrant emotions, this vivid world of marvels and miracles is expressed by Mandiargues in the calmest, most balanced prose. The look that he turns on the world around him, although it captures the excitement of existence, remains steady, calm, and untroubled. Despite the baroque luxuriance of his style, its sumptuous descriptive passages and unexpected images, it has the cadences, the simplicity, and the precise clarity of the great classical masters. Even when describing moments of ecstatic contact with the elemental forces of creation, or when depicting frenzies of sexual pleasure or sadistic torture, Mandiargues remains in total control of his means of expression, and his language never loses its cool, precise tone. His is that "lucid" delirium that he sees in Landolfi's work, the "measured excess" that he praises in Jean Paulan and of which he writes in *Troisième Belvédère*. Like the Balinese dancers whom he describes in *Le Cadran lunaire*, he proves that the height of sensual delight may be expressed without losing control, that "one can give oneself up to the greatest bodily frenzy without for all that losing possession of one's mind."

There are many examples of such calmly expressed ecstasy in Mandiargues's fiction. One of the most sustained is the scene in *La Motocyclette* in which Daniel becomes Rebecca's lover, and the pleasure that she experiences is conveyed in a measured yet intense description of the sensations that strike her. She feels that "a flame was burning in her; a certain moving, red-hued joy that she had never before felt was mingled with it." Then "she gave herself over to the pain that violently bored into her stomach, pain that changed curiously into warmth as it spread through the rest of her body." Later, as Daniel makes love to her again "she did not for one moment emerge from her state of dizzy pleasure; flakes of snow, but ones that shone with a dazzling fire and seared like puffs of steam, passed before her eyes, open in the darkness with a kind of fervor or faith, and their waves beat against her body from her eyes to her brain; each of these waves thrust her deeper beneath a marvelous mountain which was weightless even though it rose to the heavens, and which was like an immensity of absolute whiteness in the dark of the room."

The point is that Mandiargues, as an artist, knows that the mind must remain in control if he is to convey, with all the means at his disposal, the deep emotions that he feels. One might see this measured expression of ecstasy in terms of Nietzsche's view that there are two modes of perception and existence: the Apollinian and the Dionysian. In *The Birth of Tragedy*, Nietzsche describes the Apollinian as the power calmly and deliberately to create measured and harmonious beauty. The Dionysian, on the other hand, is the frenzied striving after ecstatic experience, the drunken desire to go beyond limits and bounds, the expression of the dark, impersonal will beyond the individual. It is the Dionysian mode of perception that Mandiargues's characters demonstrate in their moments of "panic" communion, but both the Apollinian and the Dionysian must be combined to achieve satisfactory expression of these feelings in a work of art.[25] It is just such a miraculous combination of two modes, the controlled expression of passion, the organization of chaos and frenzy, that Mandiargues achieves.

This tight control of himself and of his feelings enables Mandiargues to maintain close contact with the real world. The accuracy of his observation, the precision of the curious gaze that he turns on everything around and inside man, are obviously the result of a determined effort to be precise, to prevent excessive emotion from blurring the contours of his perception. To express emotion calmly, to convey abandoned frenzy accurately, to be the instrument of dark powers, yet to remain an artist in charge of one's medium is a difficult and exacting task. Mandiargues rarely fails to carry it out.

9

Mandiargues's Place in Modern Literature

IT IS PRESUMPTUOUS OF ANY CRITIC to attempt to "situate" a living writer who is at the height of his powers and still producing works of art. In this case, it is doubly presumptuous, for Mandiargues eschews categories and "schools," and has the kind of genius which it is very difficult to limit to a recognizable mold. Yet the purpose of this study is to point out some of the most important traits in his work, so it is based on the assumption that at least some general categories may be observed in it. As an introduction to his fiction, it must also, necessarily, attempt to estimate his place in contemporary French literature and his links with other modern French writers. An artist's relationship to his contemporaries is, after all, an important factor in an evaluation of his work and his techniques.

The critic's task in describing Mandiargues's place in French literature is made more difficult by the breadth of this writer's interests, his undoubted erudition, his fascination with all that is curious, beautiful, attractive, marvelous, or that, in some way, holds his attention. He has a particularly keen interest in modern art and literature, and he attempts to keep abreast of all that is valid in contemporary art, so his interests are constantly developing and expanding. At the same time, he is aware of the contribution that writers and artists of the past have made to modern art, and he shows a particular interest in the baroque, the Elizabethans, and in any work of the past that displays fantasy and imagination. His artistic and literary criticism extends from Bernini to Max Ernst, from Zurburan to Tapies, from Sade to *Le Con d'Irène;* his boundless curiosity for the unusual spectacle embraces the Mayan ruins of Palenque and the Paris Métro, the monstrous statues at Bomarzo and the dancers of Bali. His erudition touches on alchemy, mythology, astrology, archaeology, and literature in all its ramifications and obscure byways. For his wide interests (especially in the obscure and the occult), for his appreciation of modern art, and for his own production of creative works one can compare him only to the poet-critic Baudelaire, whom he calls "our perpetual hero" in *Troisième Belvédère*.

But Mandiargues is also a man of his times and has necessarily been influenced by them. Since we are concerned here with his fiction, it is as well to begin by examining how it fits into the main trends in modern fiction. Perhaps the most influential movement in this field in France since the Second World War has been the *nouveau roman*. Mandiargues, aware as always of the directions being taken by literature, has shown a keen interest in this type of novel and its practitioners. He says: "I like Sarraute and Robbe-Grillet" and he calls Ricardou "very talented."[1] Butor's novel *La Modification* is one of his favorites, for he calls it "a book that I like immensely" and adds: "But for it, perhaps I would not have written *La Motocyclette*."[2]

This comment on *La Modification* is not surprising, for both it and *La Motocyclette* use the framework of a journey to convey one person's experience of time, memories, and external reality. They put us inside an individual's consciousness and we move freely with that individual's thoughts between past, present, and future, liberated for the duration of the novel from "real time." *La Marge* too uses a rather similar technique, and all three novels present a wealth of objects and detailed descriptions of things observed in the course of a journey. We are taken on a guided tour of Barcelona, swept along the highway to Heidelberg, just as in *La Modification* we are taken by train to Rome and shown the countryside passing by, every railway station, and every physical detail of the compartment where the narrator sits. We notice and organize these things into meaningful patterns through the consciousness of the characters who experience them. Each detail, each incident is liable to provoke memories, anticipations, and reveries which we share with the characters.

This does not mean, of course, that *La Motocyclette* and *La Marge* are *nouveaux romans*, simply that Mandiargues has adapted some techniques of this genre to his own use. Although we experience time as the characters do, for example, it is made clear when we are experiencing memories or anticipation of the future. Another important difference is that the world of Robbe-Grillet, Butor, and the other writers of the *nouveau roman* remains relentlessly opaque; it assumes only the meaning that the characters impose on it. There is no pre-existing pattern in the world as they depict it. Mandiargues's world, on the other hand, is closer to Baudelaire's: it speaks to those who listen, it provides clues to the course of future events, and addresses signs to those who know how to recognize them. Nowhere in the *nouveau roman* does one have the feeling that the screen of appearances is about to be rent asunder and that the extraordinary, the impossible, and the unreal are about to spill onto the scene. Never does one feel that sense of anticipation, of things about to happen that one senses in such tales as "L'Homme du parc Monceau" or "Le passage Pommeraye." The world of the *nouveau roman* is organized according to a human consciousness, and has no power of its own. "Man looks at the world, and the world does not look back at him," says Robbe-Grillet.[3] Although Mandiargues's characters too see reality according to their own obsessions, that reality frequently escapes from their power and bends them to its will. Their world does look back at them.

The style of Mandiargues's novels is also very different from that of the *nouveau roman,* which avoids metaphor and concentrates on concrete detail. Although he picks out the details of the material world, he expresses them in a highly poetic and sometimes baroque style. Only Montherlant among modern writers shows the same sense of style, and he also shares Mandiargues's taste for the Mediterranean world. Perhaps Jacques Chessex too comes close to Mandiargues in the evocative power of his descriptions of nature and the "panic" presence in the world. As well as sensing this presence, Chessex, like Mandiargues, tends to see it as potentially hostile.

Mandiargues's use of fantasy links him to such modern writers as André Dhôtel, Marcel Béalu, and Boris Vian, although there are obvious differences of style. His depiction of a dreamlike reality in which death and desire combine, his love of German romanticism, and his fascination with magic worlds, castles, and enchanted forests all remind the reader of Julien Gracq. The combination of fantasy and the erotic suggests comparisons to Michel Bernard, while the cruel sado-erotic vein in many of his stories puts him in a stream of underground erotic literature which is well represented in France, and passes from Sade through Guillaume Apollinaire, Louis Aragon, Georges Bataille, and Pauline Réage.

Although the comparison may seem fanciful, there is also some similarity between Mandiargues's view of life and that of another important group of modern French writers: the "absurdist" philosophers. Mandiargues too sees man as separated from the world in which he lives. Rebecca, Vanina, Ferréol, and several other characters long to achieve contact with nature precisely because they are different from the rest of the created world, and they are aware of that difference. They also realize that the world is potentially hostile. Indeed, some of them are destroyed by the powers hidden in creation, and their destruction makes one think of Camus's remark: "The primitive hostility of the world throughout the millenia rises up towards us."[4] The difference, however, lies in the fact that for Camus the world is nearly always hostile, and, at best, indifferent to man. In Mandiargues's fiction, it is only hostile when men interfere with or offend the "panic" forces. Nor are his characters totally alienated in the world. Unlike the "absurdist" writers, Mandiargues believes that contact with the world is possible, that there are forces both inside us and within the world which may be united. This goes far beyond Camus's lyrical appreciation of natural beauty, for Camus believes that this beauty is totally impervious to human feelings and that nature has an existence radically different from man's.

Where Mandiargues differs most strikingly from the "absurdists," and from many other modern writers, is in his attitude to death. For Camus, Malraux, and Sartre, death is the final proof of the absurdity of existence. It dominates their novels and fills their characters with anguish. Many other writers share their attitude to death: Louis-Ferdinand Céline, Samuel Beckett, Eugène Ionesco, and Jacques Chessex to mention only a few. For Mandiargues, death is as natural a part of existence as the life forces themselves. Indeed, he sees death as one of the marvels of life, an experience to be savored as much as anything else that life offers.

Mandiargues's ability to see the marvelous everywhere, his belief that the world has hidden depths that may reveal themselves at any moment, his search for experiences that deny logic and everyday rationalistic ideals all link him firmly to surrealism. It is the surrealists whom he praises most consistently and warmly in his essays, and it is of surrealism that he says: "Everything that I have written seems more or less marked by its imprint."[5] Among the surrealists, it is Breton whom he admires the most and with whom he has the closest affinity. "I believe," he says in Le Désordre de la mémoire, "that I have been faithful to André Breton as much as or more than the other surrealists have, even if, during his lifetime, and more so every day, I have an image of him which is not in exact agreement with surrealist orthodoxy."

The bond of feeling between Mandiargues and the surrealists is due in some measure to a shared taste for certain writers and artists. Baudelaire, whom Mandiargues frequently praises, Jarry, Rimbaud, Mallarmé and Lautréamont, whom he calls in Le Cadran lunaire the "four great poets who appeared in France after Baudelaire," and the Marquis de Sade, whom he claims in Le Désordre de la mémoire to "love and admire," are all seen by the surrealists as predecessors who anticipated their own views. (Mandiargues does, however, point out in Le Désordre de la mémoire that he places Mallarmé higher than the surrealists did. Breton's appreciation of Mallarmé was intermittent, while Mandiargues has only praise for him.) The Gothic novel, which exercised a considerable influence over the surrealists, is another shared taste and Mandiargues speaks warmly of Maturin, Horace Walpole, Lewis, Anne Radcliffe, and Beckford in Le Troisième Belvédère. They also have in common their love of romanticism. Aragon claimed that the surrealists had made romanticism known again in France,[6] but it was what J. H. Matthews calls the "exacerbated stage" of romanticism that they particu-

larly liked: the works of Petrus Borel, Théophile Dondey, Aloysius Ber-
trand, and Nerval.[7] They admired the German romantics too—Jean-Paul,
Novalis and Hölderlin in particular. In *Le Désordre de la mémoire*, Mandiargues makes it clear that his favorites are romantics of the same tendencies, especially Nerval and Nodier, and he also reserves high praise
for the German romantics, pointing out that he took a copy of Hölderlin's
Poems of Madness everywhere with him for several years. Even Mandiargues's love of what is modern is shared with the surrealists, who, in 1922,
organized an International Congress for the Determining of Directives
and Defense of the Modern Spirit.

     In their artistic theory and practice, and in their general at-
titudes, Mandiargues and the surrealists are often indistinguishable. They
both praise and use fantasy in their art, seeing it as a means of liberating
man's imagination from the shackles of cold logic. In Mandiargues's
fiction, unsuspected possibilities open before the reader's eyes, fantasy
liberates the mind from logical thought, and the imagination is set free.
When reading his tales, one is reminded of Breton's remark: "Only at the
gates of the fantastic, at the point where human reason loses control, do
the deepest emotions of one's being have every chance of being realized,
emotions which cannot emerge freely in the framework of the real world,
and which, in their very haste, have no other outlet, but in the form of
response to the eternal temptation of symbols and myth."[8] Mandiargues
attacks the stable, fixed nature of the world by changing the conditions
under which it normally operates. He makes characters change shape and
size, transports them to other domains, alters the flow of time, and makes
dream project into reality. By so doing, he fulfills one of the main aims of
surrealism, which is, in the words of J. H. Matthews, to use "distortion,
transformation, metamorphosis—anything in fact that resists the perni-
ciously stable nature of the universe as we know it."[9]

     For the surrealists, another way of liberating the imagination was
by use of the marvelous, and they attempted, in their writing and their
paintings, to show it hidden in the world around us. As one critic puts it,
they believed that: "The true purpose of art and indeed of life itself was to
expand our definition of reality until it included the marvelous."[10] Mandiargues more than once expresses similar ideas, pointing out that the
unexpected may be found in the tiny details of life, the objects that
surround us, the events that we take for granted. In his fiction, Vanina
finds the marvelous in a flower, Rebecca discovers it in a motorcycle,
Pascal Bénin in a stone.

     The marvelous and the hidden face of the world were often re-
vealed to the surrealists by what they called "objective chance." They
believed that chance events could suddenly plunge them into the world of
the surreal, as when Breton, quite by chance, met Nadja, or when he

discovered, in a Paris flea-market, an object which seemed to speak to him in some mysterious way. We have already noted at least two such events in Mandiargues's own life: the incidents of the child in the painting and the calf's head under the Bridge of Sighs. In his fiction, it is this "objective chance" that leads Pascal Bénin to pick up the stone that causes his death, that impels the narrator of "Le passage Pommeraye" to enter the sidestreet, and that brings together Ferréol Buq and the old man who guides him to the death ceremony. Often, as in the case of Breton and Nadja, it is a woman who is sent by fate. She is the instrument of the marvelous for Mandiargues, since she reveals the essence of life and death (the dying woman in *Marbre*), lures the hero to undertake mysterious journeys ("Le passage Pommeraye" from *Le Musée noir* and "L'Opéra des falaises" from *Soleil des loups*), acts as the vehicle of dreams and revelations (the prostitutes in "La Grotte" from *Porte dévergondée* and "L'Enfantillage" from *Feu de braise*), and is the receptacle of the life forces (Vanina, Rebecca, and Sarah). Mandiargues, when he depicts woman as the vehicle of the marvelous and says in *Le Désordre de la mémoire* that she is, for him, "together with poetry, my most powerful mobilizer of emotion," is in a surrealist tradition. The surrealists too saw woman as the projection of marvel and beauty into life, and this is the role of Heide in Gracq's *Au Château d'Argol*, of Mona in Jouffroy's *Un Rêve plus long que la nuit*, and of the women in Eluard's and Breton's poetry.

Woman is often seen by the surrealists as an instrument of the marvelous because she inspires love. The same is true of Mandiargues, whose words in *Le Désordre de la mémoire* that love is "the great reason for living" echo Breton's: "There is no solution except love."[11] Although love plays a lesser role in Mandiargues's work than eroticism, there is no doubt that, in his life, it has played a critical part. His love for Bona, described in *Bona l'amour et la peinture*, is depicted as a *coup de foudre*, a poetic and idealized love that changed his life as does *l'amour fou* in surrealist mythology. This love is the inspiration of much of his poetry, as it is of Breton's, Eluard's and Aragon's.

In addition to love of this kind, both Mandiargues and the surrealists recognize the importance of desire. Breton talks of "desire, the only incentive in the world, desire, the only rigor that man need know."[12] By desire, the surrealists often mean the uninhibited expression of sexual passion, and this is, of course, one of the things that they admire in Sade. It is not *just* that, however. It is the will to break out of one's limits, to destroy logical categories, to go beyond appearances, and to possess more than one is normally able to possess in this life. Judith Reigl expresses this kind of desire when she says: "The essential basis of all creative activity is the despairing desire to destroy the contradictions and the limits of personal existence, both human and universal, to grow in extent thanks to a permanent revolt."[13] Mandiargues clearly demonstrates both kinds of desire in his writing. The sexual variety is evident in the vein of sado-eroticism in nearly all his fiction which culminates in the scenes of sexual excess in *L'Anglais décrit dans le château fermé*. The desire to escape the limits of self, either in erotic abandon or in "panic" experience has also been described in some detail. It is sufficient at this point to remind the reader of the furious desire for the world experienced by many of his characters, the longing to merge with nature that culminates in "panic" communion.

The same will to shock lies behind much of the uncontrolled eroticism of the surrealists and of Mandiargues's writings. They attempt to scandalize, to flout bourgeois morals, and to shake people out of rigidly set attitudes. The anti-conformism that surrealism inherited from Dada is precisely one of the things that endears both movements to Mandiargues, and he has said in *Le Désordre de la mémoire* that, "like any surrealist worthy of that name, I am naturally disrespectful." He and the surrealists believe that the tension created by unconventional attitudes, and especially by sexual excess, adds excitement and power to a work of art. It is, as Bataille (who was also associated with surrealism) points out, the sense of transgression that makes eroticism such a powerful force.[14]

In view of our earlier examination of the similarity between Mandiargues's attitude toward material reality and that of the surrealists, only a brief reminder is necessary here. Mandiargues insists on accurate detail in his description of the world around him, and, as he himself points out, this is also true of the surrealists.[15] This similarity of technique is due to a shared vision of the objects of reality. Surrealism takes objects, observed in all their detail, and removes them from their utilitarian context. When they are placed in a new context, in proximity with things not normally associated with them, new potential is released in them. Mandiargues recommends the same method, and he speaks, in a passage from *Le Belvédère* mentioned in the previous chapter, of the resonances set up when an object such as Bernini's statue of Louis XIV is placed in unusual surroundings. The statue that Férreol Buq finds on the deserted island, the ruins in the midst of the Mexican jungle described in *Deuxième Belvédère*, the insect scuttling across his desk at the beginning of *Marbre* are just a few examples of how Mandiargues, in his own work, shows us objects which interact in unusual ways with their surroundings.

He is also fascinated, like the surrealists, by objects found by chance which capture the finder's imagination and which meet some kind of unconscious need. The wooden spoon and the mask found by Breton and Giacometti in a Paris flea-market are the best known examples of this phenomenon. They served as a catalyst to free the artists' imagination, just as the insect, the paperweight, and the list of names inspired *Marbre*.

For all these artists, objects speak and affect the behavior of men. Hence, in Mandiargues's work, the objects in the shop window have an effect on the narrator of "Le passage Pommeraye" *(Le Musée noir)*, the furniture in the château seems to take over the narrator's thoughts in "La Vision capitale" *(Soleil des loups)*, and the Columbus Monument suggests to Sigismond how he should combat death.

The surrealists believe that the world speaks to man in other ways too. Although they reject orthodox religion, they see man as manipulated by forces greater than himself, forces that may suddenly communicate with him. Just before he fell asleep one night, Breton became aware of a sentence unexpectedly entering his mind: "There is a man cut in two by the window."[16] We are familiar with such messages from obscure forces in Mandiargues's fiction: the phrase "the burden of destiny" that imprints itself on the consciousness of the narrator of "Le passage Pommeraye"; the words "When the girl had entered the wood, the unknown seized her," that come to Vanina as she goes off in search of the young man. There is also the sentence quoted in *Bona l'amour et la peinture:* "There are beautiful October days in Paris" that came to Mandiargues shortly before he met Bona for the first time.

For the surrealists, the artist is merely an instrument, a medium through which forces such as these may speak. They downplay the role of creativity and emphasize the artist as a transmitter of secret forces. This is particularly true when the forces in question come from *inside* the artist. They believe that the artist has to be in a particular state of mind in order to produce works, and that he must not let his rational faculties interfere with the process. The attraction of automatism is that it allows them to express what lies deep inside them without the restraint of reason. Their interest in dreams has a similar basis, for, in the process of dreaming, the depths of the psyche are released without the interference of the dreamer, who is just a passive instrument.

Mandiargues has also talked of the artist as a medium, and has, on occasions, practiced a kind of automatic writing. He believes too that it is necessary to be in a particular state of mind in order to create. His interest in dreams is at least as keen as that of the surrealists, and is based partly on the belief that they reveal the inner recesses of the self. Like Breton, Mandiargues would like dreams and reverie to affect reality, to change the course of events, and in such tales as "Le Marronnier" and "Le Triangle ambigu" (both from *Mascarets*) this is what happens. He also sees dreams as a means of enriching his writing and of making it appeal on a kind of subliminal level at which dream images and symbols operate.

The surrealist attempt to project dreams into life, to liberate the inner self, to reconcile what lies inside us with life outside all show a desire to bring together the forces within us and the ones that direct our waking life. This is also the goal of many of Mandiargues's characters, and it is achieved by Vanina, Rebecca, and others when they experience "panic" communion with the universe. Dream, reverie, the mysterious forces of life within and without us all mingle in Mandiargues's fiction to achieve that surreality which is the goal of surrealist art.

In addition to these similarities of aims, attitudes and techniques, there are, naturally enough, certain motifs and recurring situations in Mandiargues's work that may be considered typically surrealist. The surrealists are, for example, fascinated by castles (and this may possibly reflect the influence of the Gothic novel on their sensibility). Castles appear in Gracq's *Au Château d'Argol*, in Maurice Fourré's *Tête-de-nègre*, and are often mentioned by Breton. Mandiargues sets *L'Anglais décrit dans le château fermé* in an isolated castle, as well as the culminating scene of "La Vision capitale." Damien visits Camille de Hur in her castle, and Frederick II's Castel del Monte is the subject of "L'Espion des Pouilles" in *Le Cadran lunaire*. The delight that surrealists show in museums and collections of unusual objects finds its echo in the museum that Sigismond visits in *La Marge*, the one where Conrad Mur sees the wax statue, and the strange collection made by Father Athanase in *Marbre*. The markets that exercised such fascination for Breton, because of the possibility of finding an interesting object there, can also be found in Mandiargues's work, for example the market that Sigismond visits in Barcelona, and the one described in "Les Marchés du Temple" in *Le Cadran lunaire*. One story, "Le passage Pommeraye," depicts a street that is very reminiscent of the passage de L'Opéra, the setting of Aragon's *Le Paysan de Paris*.[17] Indeed, the idea of "passage" conveyed by both these stories is a common surrealist concept. The surrealist motif of a passage or link between this world and the one of surreality is reflected in the bridges, corridors, and streets of many of Mandiargues's stories.

We are obviously dealing here, not so much with an "influence" exercised by surrealism, as with a shared sensibility. Of all the trends in modern French literature, this is the one with which Mandiargues has the most affinity. Yet he did break with the group, was associated with it for only a few years, and was just peripherally involved in its activity. He *is* a surrealist in many ways, but not entirely so. He is too independent, too determined to be bound by no imperatives, too much an individual to belong completely in any one group. His genius cannot be limited to one set of theories and practices, however much sympathy he has with them. He has said: "But many of my writings are not surrealist-oriented. My styles differ with my moods, my ideas, according to the inspiration of the moment."[18] Paradoxically, Mandiargues is never more a surrealist than when he affirms the spirit of freedom and revolt, and takes his leave of surrealism.

One major point on which he parts company with them is their attitude toward the artist. Although he has used techniques similar to automatism, and although he sees the artist as a medium and a *voyant,* he does not have the surrealists' disregard for the artist's creativity. The logical consequence of belief in the passivity of the artist is the idea that little creative activity is involved in producing works of art. In J. H. Matthews's words: "Automatic practices . . . are not submitted to any interference from aesthetic considerations."[19] Mandiargues's comment in *Troisième Belvédère* that the novelist is a dreamer "sustained by the gift or the acquisition of a style" shows that he believes the writer is not *just* a medium: he must also fashion his dreams and inspiration into something stylish. The artist's will has a part in the creation of works of art in his opinion. Discussing the use of dreams in the creation of a poem, he says: "Will . . . plays a certain role in that dream. It is, in a way, a guided dream. And so, it is in the use that one makes of it that it takes the form of art."[20] The tight control that Mandiargues exercises over his medium, the careful, calm, and deliberate balance of his prose show that he does not simply let inspiration pour through him. His evocation of dream, passion, ecstasy, and the black demons of the self is cunningly and consciously done.

Another point on which Mandiargues takes issue with the surrealists is their hermeticism. They often seem, in his opinion, to scorn the public at large and to see any attempt to appeal to a wider group of readers as being sordidly commercial. He argues that they share Mallarmé's belief that "a respectable writer must ruin his publisher and that the mass of people are stupid."[21] He himself thinks that more and more people have open and inquiring minds, and are interested in the avant-garde. It is the artist's duty to appeal to as many of these potential readers as possible.

One thing that makes Mandiargues's work more accessible than many surrealist writings is that much of it is fiction. Although some of the surrealists wrote novels, they generally affected great scorn for fiction. They saw the novel in particular as subservient to logic, to rational development of character and of plot. It pandered, they believed, to bourgeois tastes for rational categories. When they do turn their hands to novel writing, the result tends to be works with little concern for the logical development and plot of traditional novels. Mandiargues's fiction, although it often has a rather thin plot, nevertheless has one, and a recognizable story line is developed. He is aware of this difference from the surrealists, who, he says, "had no interest in the novel with a plot, and [who] usually rejected invented narrative." He adds: "I am not so rigorous and I consider invention one of the main qualities of the storyteller."[22]

Linked with the surrealists' dislike of the novel was their scorn for "literature." They placed poetry higher than all else, and professed only contempt for other forms of literary expression, especially when in a traditional mold. Mandiargues was never able to reconcile himself to this distinction, for his tastes are wide enough to embrace many of those who do not figure in the surrealists' pantheon of "acceptable" writers. Just as Soupault and Artaud were eventually excluded by Breton because they admitted to a belief in the value of literary activity, so Mandiargues had to break with the surrealists when he expressed admiration for René de Solier's literary qualities. Mandiargues is too much of a literary craftsman himself to accept this attitude, and he points out in *Le Désordre de la mémoire* that many products of surrealist writing are themselves literature anyway.

Perhaps Mandiargues's relationship to the surrealists may best be seen as a sharing of certain attitudes that have always existed. Surrealism is a complex of beliefs and ways of looking at the world which are timeless, and which existed before the term "surrealism" was coined. Breton has said that "surrealism, from its beginning, presented itself as the codification of a state of mind that has shown itself sporadically in all ages and in all countries."[23] Mandiargues holds many of the same attitudes, and saw in the surrealists *frères d'élection* with whom he could sympathize. The movement was never viewed by him as a series of beliefs to which he must rigidly adhere. In fact, although he may share some of the surrealists' attitudes, there are certain others, just as old, which form an integral part of his work. These are his mythical beliefs.

The language of myth is an ancient one that still finds expression in Mandiargues's fiction. As Jung has pointed out, the symbols and language of myth are also those that the unconscious uses to express itself in dreams. One striking feature of both dreams and myth is that the same basic themes, images, and symbols appear in widely separated cultures. This has led Jung to posit the existence of a collective unconscious, which exists in addition to the individual's unconscious, and which is part of the heritage of all mankind. Our brain, he argues, has been shaped and influenced by the experiences of our ancestors, producing an unconscious containing "primordial images which have always been the basis of man's thinking—the whole treasure house of mythological motifs."[24] These inborn forms of the unconscious are called "archetypes" by Jung, and it is these, according to his theory, which form the typical images of myth and dream.

It is not within the scope of this book to discuss the validity of Jung's theories, but the images released in dream and myth do seem to come from deep within the human psyche. Dream and myth may be the remnants of a primitive way of thought, an early system of language that still persists in the unconscious. Mircea Eliade refers to that part of us which bears such images in it as the nonhistorical part of man, for it goes back to a time before history and remains unchanged by the passage of time. He writes: "The nonhistorical part of the human being wears, like a medal, the imprinted memories of a richer, a more complete and almost beautiful existence."[25]

Mandiargues's art, while belonging to this time and resembling in some ways the works of several other contemporary writers, attempts to go back to the very beginning of human thought and to tap this nonhistorical part of the psyche. It is quite possible that the part of the human mind to which Eliade refers bears "imprinted" images. We know that animals have such imprints, which are not learned, and which provoke immediate response to various stimuli. When an animal responds this way, it does not do so as an individual animal, but as part of a species that must react in a certain way. The images and symbols of myth seem to provoke the same kind of reactions in the human mind, reactions common to the whole species. The experiences which structure myth and produce these symbols are ones that all men share, such as birth, death, sundering from the maternal breast, and the realization of the difference between sexes. They are such fundamental, potentially traumatic experiences that the images associated with them never lose their effect; they work almost as stimuli to the nervous system. Writing of these symbols, one Jungian psychologist says: "These images seem to possess a power and energy of their own—they move and speak, they perceive and have purposes—they fascinate us and drive us to action which is entirely against our conscious intention."[26]

It is obvious that any artist who uses the symbolic language of myth and dream has an instrument of immense power at his command. His art could touch us at a primordial, unconscious level, releasing responses that defy logic. Any art does this to some extent, for art appeals at a level beyond rational processes. As Campbell says: "Art is not, like science, a logic of references, but a release from reference and rendition of immediate experience: a presentation of forms, images, or ideas in such a way that they will communicate, nor primarily a thought or even a feeling, but an impact."[27] How much truer this is of an art that deliberately uses dream and myth, as does Mandiargues's. The fascination, the dreamlike web of enchantment spun in his tales must be due in large measure to his ability to manipulate the symbols and language that speak to us on this unconscious level.

Mandiargues is well aware of the power that such an art may exercise. In *Troisième Belvédère* he attributes the fascination of certain paintings, such as those of the Fontainebleau School, to their use of "archetypes, figures of universal dream common to all men." In *Deuxième Belvédère* he says that modern artists such as Tapies and Chirico provoke deep responses because they are able "to bring into the light forms and memories buried in the deepest layers of memory." He is equally aware that he himself applies similar techniques, and, among his works, he singles out *La Motocyclette* as operating on this level. What he says about that one novel might apply to all that he has ever written: "These are dream images, rather like what Jung calls 'deep archetypes,' which come to the surface at certain moments and which, in my opinion, add to the poetic or dramatic intensity of a story."[28]

The surrealists too used dreams in order to communicate on this level; they practiced automatism in order to release symbols and images that might speak to the collective unconscious. They even showed an interest in myth, and such works as Gracq's *Au Château d'Argol* may be seen as a mythical quest.[29] But none of these writers is doing anything very new: they are merely expressing a traditional way of looking at life that goes back a long time in literature. Myth and mythic structures have been used by writers from Dante to Joyce, from Bunyan's *The Pilgrim's Progess* to Lewis's *The Lion, the Witch and the Wardrobe*, from Arthurian romance to Adams's *Shardik*. Dreams and dreamlike experience have formed the basis of innumerable works of fiction from the *Matière de Bretagne* to *Alice in Wonderland*. Mandiargues's art is part of a very old tradition.

He naturally uses the language of myth because his view of the forces at work in the world, and of man's relationship to them, is identical with that of ancient myth. Although his fiction appears, at first glance, to be only lighthearted fantasy, there is more to it than that. His fantasy is deliberately worked into certain recurring patterns, the strange events in his works are repeated, the ritualistic situations reappear, the same metamorphoses overtake his characters, time follows similar unusual paths because Mandiargues is expressing a particular view of life in all his fiction. He molds his fantasy to the same mythical patterns because these are the patterns that best express his view of human existence. Fantasy in Mandiargues's work is not the equivalent of frivolity; it is used to tell us something about the nature of life.

Myth conveys in symbolic language truths that are not comprehensible by logic alone, and Mandiargues tries to convey the same incomprehensible truths as myth. His heroes discover these inexplicable realities because they are willing, like the heroes of myth, to leave the security of everyday life and face trials and ordeals. There is a movement from a limited, inhibiting (though often comfortable) social setting towards a wider world of secrets that encompass the whole of humanity. This represents a rupture, not just with a particular social setting, but with a whole complex of inhibiting attitudes. As Campbell puts it, "the rupture is rather with the comparatively trivial attitude toward both the human spirit and the world that appears to satisfy the great majority."[30]

Mandiargues's fiction cannot be defined entirely by its relationship to other contemporary artists, trends, and movements. Because of its
striking similarity to the archetypal myth, it appeals to part of the human
mind which is timeless and which still thinks in certain "primitive" patterns. By appealing to this part of us, Mandiargues invites us to reject the
"trivial attitude" to which Campbell refers; he invites us to abandon the
superficial view of life that looks no further than appearances and to
travel, as the mythical hero does, to another realm of perception. Here
we will discover truths that are best conveyed in mythical terms; we will
see those forces that, according to myth, surround and inhabit us all the
time; we will become aware of the beauty and mystery of life; we will
know a world that opens and speaks to us. This is the "message" hidden in
his work. The function of the recurring motifs and themes in Mandiargues's fiction is to provide us with a way of looking at the world with new
eyes.

Notes

INTRODUCTION

1. These incidents may be found in "Le Pain rouge," *Soleil des loups* (Paris: Laffont, 1951), pp. 107–132; "Le Diamant," *Feu de braise* (Paris: Grasset, 1959), pp. 143–186; "L'Archéologue," *Soleil des loups*, pp. 7–94; "Le passage Pommeraye," *Le Musée noir* (Paris: Folio, 1974), pp. 89–117; "L'Opéra des falaises," *Soleil des loups*, pp. 171–208; "L'Etudiante," *Soleil des loups*, pp. 133–170; "Les Pierreuses," *Feu de braise*, pp. 53–68.

2. These quotations are taken, respectively, from Jean d'Ormesson, "André Pieyre de Mandiargues entre l'art et l'amour," *Les Nouvelles Littéraires*, 14 mai 1971, p. 6; Matthias-E. Korger, "André Pieyre de Mandiargues et la métamorphose du romantisme," *Marginales* 121 (juillet 1968): 5; Claude Bonnefoy, "André Pieyre de Mandiargues," in *Dictionnaire de la littérature française contemporaine*, edited by Claude Bonnefoy, Tony Cartano, and Daniel Oster (Paris: Jean-Pierre Delarge, 1977), p. 254; Alain Clerval, "André Pieyre de Mandiargues: un érotique baroque," *La Nouvelle Revue Française* 38 (août 1971): 77; André Gascht, "André Pieyre de Mandiargues, un réaliste de l'imaginaire," *Biblio* 34 (novembre 1966): 4; Mark J. Temmer, "André Pieyre de Mandiargues," *Yale French Studies* 31 (1964): 99.

3. Taken, respectively, from Bonnefoy, "Mandiargues," p. 253; André Gascht, "un réaliste de l'imaginaire," p. 4; Robert Kanters, "André Pieyre de Mandiargues et la mort en suspens," *Le Figaro Littéraire*, 5–11 juin 1967, p. 19; Robert Abirached, "D'un merveilleux moderne," *La Nouvelle Revue Française* 21 (juin 1963): 1075; André Robin, "André Pieyre de Mandiargues ou l'initiation panique I: La perversité cosmique," *Cahiers du Sud* 60, nos. 383–4 (août–septembre–octobre 1965): 138; Marc Alyn, "André Pieyre de Mandiargues: L'Age de craie," *Table Ronde* 172 (mai 1962): 120; Peter Brooks, "The Pleasure Principle," *Partisan Review* 33 (Winter 1966): 128; Robert Kanters, "André Pieyre de Mandiargues," *La Revue de Paris* 75, no. 1 (janvier 1968): 116; Gascht, "un réaliste de l'imaginaire," p. 3.

4. Quoted by Francine Mallet, "Des *Années sordides* à *La Marge*, l'œuvre de Pieyre de Mandiargues enrichit les mêmes thèmes," *Le Monde [des Livres]*, 3 mai 1967, p. 1.

5. Octavio Paz, *Alternating Current*, trans. Helen R. Lane (New York: Viking, 1973), p. 92; d'Ormesson, "entre l'art et l'amour," p. 6; Kanters, "Mandiargues," p. 123.

6. There is one published study of his poetry: Salah Stétié, *André Pieyre de Mandiargues* (Paris: Seghers, 1978).

7. In an earlier article, I have already pointed out what most of these patterns are. See "Recurring Patterns of Fantasy in the Fiction of André Pieyre de Mandiargues," *Symposium* 39 (Spring–Summer 1975): 30–47.

8. Marcel Schneider, *La Littérature fantastique en France* (Paris: Fayard, 1964), p. 9.

9. This association is discussed in more detail in chapter 1. However, Mandiar-

gues's own account may be read in *Le Désordre de la mémoire* (Paris: Gallimard, 1975), pp. 108–111, 132, 135; and in Bettina Knapp, "André Pieyre de Mandiargues," in *French Novelists Speak Out*, edited by Bettina Knapp (Troy, N.Y.: Whitston, 1976), pp. 48–49.

10. Alain Jouffroy, "Entretien: Mandiargues, celui qui a fait peur aux jurys," *L'Express*, 6 décembre 1963, p. 44.

11. André Pieyre de Mandiargues, "D'Aurélia à Mona," *L'Express*, 7 novembre 1963, p. 44.

1—A BIOGRAPHICAL SKETCH

1. Most of the biographical information contained in this chapter is to be found in *Le Désordre de la mémoire* (Paris: Gallimard, 1975), an invaluable source of information on Mandiargues's life, opinions, likes, dislikes, and personal attitudes. I have also used, to a much lesser extent, *Bona l'amour et la peinture* (Geneva: Skira, 1971). All quotations in this chapter, unless otherwise specified, are from *Le Désordre de la mémoire*.

2. It must be pointed out that, despite the way the men characters treat many of the women in his work, Mandiargues has always defended women as individuals and human beings who should have the same rights as men. In *Bona l'amour et la peinture* he reacts violently against critics who reject women artists merely because they are women, and he describes the *code napoléon*, which discriminates against women, as "a sinisterly named code, a code devised by swine."

3. Preface to *L'Age de craie* (Paris: Gallimard, 1967), p. 8.

4. Bettina Knapp, "André Pieyre de Mandiargues," in *French Novelists Speak Out*, edited by Bettina Knapp (Troy, N.Y.: Whitson, 1976), p. 54.

5. Marcel Arland, "Les Contes fantastiques de Pieyre de Mandiargues," in *Nouvelles Lettres de France* (Paris: Albin Michel, 1954), pp. 60 and 62.

6. Arland, "Les Contes fantastiques," p. 58; Gerda Zeltner, *La Grande aventure du roman français au XXᵉ siècle* (Paris: Société Nouvelle des Editions Gonthier, 1967), p. 125; Robert Poulet, "Suite et fin des faits nouveaux," *Ecrits de Paris*, avril 1969, p. 95.

7. Roger Nimier, "André Pieyre de Mandiargues," in *Journées de lectures* (Paris: Gallimard, 1965), p. 227.

8. Henri Rode, "Les Romans et les jours," *Marginales* 52 (février 1957): 53.

9. André Robin, "André Pieyre de Mandiargues ou l'initiation panique II: L'Initiation panique," *Cahiers du Sud* 60, no. 385 (novembre–décembre 1965): 296.

10. André Gascht, "André Pieyre de Mandiargues, un réaliste de l'imaginaire," *Biblio* 34 (novembre 1966): 6.

11. Christian Dedet, "André Pieyre de Mandiargues, *La Motocyclette*," *La Table Ronde* 193 (février 1964): 142.

12. Peter Brooks, "The Pleasure Principle," *Partisan Review* 33, no. 1 (Winter 1966): 130.

13. According to Francine Mallet, "Des *Années Sordides* à *La Marge*, l'œuvre de Pieyre de Mandiargues enrichit les mêmes thèmes," *Le Monde* [*des Livres*], 3 mai 1967, p. i.

14. Pierre Gamarra, "Les Livres nouveaux," *Europe*, nos. 465–66 (janvier–février 1968): 241.

15. C. T., "Dropping Out in All Directions," *Observer*, 1 February 1970, p. 30.

16. Quotations and information in this paragraph are from a personal letter by Pieyre de Mandiargues to the author.

17. Borowcyzk has also made films of *La Marge* and "Le Sang de l'agneau," while Jacqueline Audry has made a film of *Le Lis de mer*.

18. Alain Clerval, "André Pieyre de Mandiargues: un érotique baroque," *La Nouvelle Revue Française* 38 (août 1971): 79.

19. Arnold de Kerchove, "René Fallet, Louise de Vilmorin et André Pieyre de Manidargues," *Revue Générale* 8 (1971): 109; and Alain Clerval, "un érotique baroque," p. 78.

2—EROS AND PAN

1. André Pieyre de Mandiargues, "Hans Bellmer: Anatomie de l'image," *La Nouvelle Nouvelle Revue Française* 10 (novembre 1957): 973.

2. These scenes are to be found in, respectively, "Le Sang de l'agneau," *Le Musée noir* (Paris: Folio, 1974), pp. 15–88; *La Motocyclette* (Paris: Folio, 1973); *Isabella Morra* (Paris: Gallimard, 1973); "Mil neuf cent trente-trois," *Sous la lame* (Paris: Gallimard, 1976), pp. 7–76.

3. It has been rumored that Mandiargues is the author of the erotic novel *Histoire d'O*, published under the name of Pauline Réage. He denies this story, however, and attributes the rumor to Jean Paulhan. See *Le Désordre de la mémoire* (Paris: Gallimard, 1975), pp. 173–74.

4. For these theories, see Georges Bataille, *L'Erotisme* (Paris: Les Editions de Minuit, 1957), pp. 71–90.

5. In "Le Marronnier," from *Mascarets* (Paris: Gallimard, 1971), pp. 29–60, a man dreams of sexual relations with one of the women characters, while they sit beneath a tree, set inside a circular space, which is itself set within a square garden. As though taking part in some religious ritual, they pass a marijuana cigarette from one person to another. In "Armoire de lune" (*Mascarets*, pp. 93–108), two characters take part in a grim ritual performed on a tomb, while in "La Révélation"(*Mascarets*, pp. 151–71), the male character visits a woman who lives in a house which resembles a converted church. "Le Nu parmi les cercueils," from *Feu de braise* (Paris: Grasset, 1959), pp. 91–141, tells of a woman made to perform a ritual striptease while surrounded by a circle of coffins.

6. Other sacrificial victims are Sarah Mose in "Le Diamant" (*Feu de braise*, pp. 143–86), who assumes a crucified position as she couples with a lion-man inside a diamond; the girl in "Armoire de lune," who, before she will give herself to the man, seeks "the ideal spot to give herself up to a sacrifice" (*Mascarets*, p. 99); the prostitute in "La Grotte," from *Porte dévergondée* (Paris: Gallimard, 1965), pp. 47–96, whom the male character imagines lying naked on a rock, her arms chained to pillars on either side; Isabella Morra, from the play of that name, who is sacrificially killed by her brothers.

7. In "Le Diamant," Sarah undertakes a fast and ritual cleansing before she becomes a sacrifice.

8. See "Le Diamant," "Sabine" (*Porte dévergondée*, pp. 17–45), and "Armoire de lune." See also the article "En Souvenir de Trieste" in *Troisième Belvédère* (Paris: Gallimard, 1971), pp. 227–33, where Mandiargues talks of the importance of the theme of defloration in the works of the Italian writer Quarantotti Gambini.

9. This is also, of course the name of her husband, who is something of a nonentity.

10. Union with the mineral world is even more obviously achieved in "Le Diamant," in which Sarah Mose shrinks in size and is absorbed by a diamond.

11. Communion with the animal world is also linked to the erotic in two other stories. In "Adive" (*Mascarets*, pp. 109–49), a woman has an erotic experience provoked by a dog, while in "Rodogune" (*Feu de braise*, pp. 23–51) it is hinted, but never proved, that the heroine has sexual relations with her pet ram.

12. See Mircea Eliade, *Images and Symbols. Studies in Religious Symbolism* (New York: Sheed and Ward, 1969), pp. 44–47, 163.

13. There are other examples in Mandiargues's work of the woman serving as the instrument of communion. In "La Grotte" (*Porte dévergondée*, pp. 47–96), a man uses a prostitute to help him create a reverie in which he enters the mineral world through a grotto. "Le pont" (*Le Musée noir*, pp. 247–83) describes how a man achieves "panic" communion through sexual relations with a woman whom he meets in a wood. In "Le Marronnier," the woman with whom one of the men wants to have sexual relations is herself the forces of nature, for she is called Cérès.

14. The sexual connotations of the seashore seem to be connected with an incident in Mandiargues's adolescence described in *Le Désordre de la mémoire*, pp. 84–86. It appears that he was walking along the seashore, in a state of intense sexual excitement, when he met a young girl. Exposing himself to her, he ejaculated before her, then bathed his penis in the sea and went calmly home.

15. "En écho," from *Le Point où j'en suis suivi de Dalila exaltée et de La Nuit l'amour* (Paris: Gallimard, 1964), p. 79.

16. See "La Griffe de Max Ernst," *Deuxième Belvédère* (Paris: Grasset, 1962), pp. 139–52; "C'est assez beau comme ça," *Troisième Belvédère*, pp. 11–42; "Les Matériologies," *Deuxième Belvédère*, pp. 183–87; "Dubuffet à Londres," "Toledo hors de pair," "Les Aigrettes du langage," *Troisième Belvédère*, pp. 53–56; 91–94; 263–68; "Germaine Richier," *Le Belvédère*, pp. 21–32.

3—EROS AND THANATOS

1. André Breton, *Nadja* (Paris: Gallimard, 1928), p. 53.

2. In "L'Archéologue" from *Soleil des loups* (Paris: Laffont, 1951), pp. 8–93, the hero is transported in a dream to the sea bed where he is plunged into a timeless world. This story will be examined in more detail later.

3. "Le Casino patibulaire" from *Le Musée noir* (Paris: Folio, 1974), pp. 285–305, also tells of a man who suddenly realizes that he is living the events of a dream that he had the night before.

4. Thomas Mann, "Freud and the Future," *Essays of Three Decades*, translated by H.T. Lowe-Porter (New York: Knopf, 1947), p. 416.

5. It should also be pointed out that one other story, "Clorinde" (*Soleil des loups*, pp. 95–106), is very similar. It tells how a man discovers a tiny female creature in the woods and is seized with desire for her. Unable to consummate his desire, since she is so small, he rushes off and leaves her. When he comes back, she has disappeared, and the man realizes that he is condemned to die.

6. In "Le Casino patibulaire" there is a similar incident. The hero has a dream in which he approaches an altar with a veiled bride at his side. When he lifts her veil, he discovers a rotting bovine head.

7. See Joseph Campbell, *The Hero With a Thousand Faces* (Princeton: Princeton University Press, 1972), pp. 26–27.

8. "Alfonso Reyes," *La Nouvelle Nouvelle Revue Française* 15 (février 1960): 346.

4—ESCAPE FROM THE SELF

1. Georges Bataille, *L'Erotisme* (Paris: Les Editions de Minuit, 1957), p. 155.

2. This is related in *Le Désordre de la mémoire* (Paris: Gallimard, 1975), pp. 90–91.

3. André Pieyre de Mandiargues, Preface to *Les Masques de Léonor Fini* (Paris: La Parade, 1951). Pages not numbered. Italics in original.

4. André Pieyre de Mandiargues, *Les Masques de Léonor Fini*. Italics in original.

5. Conrad Mur in "L'Archéologue," from *Soleil des loups* (Paris: Laffont, 1951), pp. 7–93, also descends under water and finds himself in a world where his usual environment has changed.

6. Bataille, *L'Erotisme*, p. 250.

7. Ibid, p. 126.

8. He talks of astrology in "Parler de l'astrologie," from *Troisième Belvédère* (Paris: Gallimard, 1971), pp. 135–39, and in *Le Désordre de la mémoire* (Paris: Gallimard, 1975), pp.116–17.

9. For a study of Mandiargues's fiction as a mystic endeavor, see my article "Mystic and Erotic Experience in the Fiction of André Pieyre de Mandiargues," *Kentucky Romance Quarterly* 28, no. 2 (1980): 205–13.

10. Quoted by Bettina Knapp, "André Pieyre de Mandiargues," in *French Novelists Speak Out*, edited by Bettina Knapp (Troy, N.Y.: Whitston, 1976), pp. 52–53.

11. Alain Jouffroy, "Entretien: Mandiargues, celui qui a fait peur aux jurys," *L'Express*, 6 décembre 1963, p. 44.

12. See *Le Belvédère* (Paris: Grasset, 1958), p. 156.

13. See *Troisième Belvédère*, pp. 48, 90, and 111–12.

14. Quoted by Bettina Knapp, "André Pieyre de Mandiargues," p. 52.

15. Susan Campanini, "Alchemy in Pieyre de Mandiargues's 'Le Diamant'," *French Review* 50, no. 4 (March 1977): 602–9.

16. Mandiargues's interest in alchemy is expressed in several places. See, for example, *Deuxième Belvédère* (Paris: Grasset, 1962), p. 186; *Troisième Belvédère*, pp. 37, 39, 103, 290, and 291.

17. Anna Balakian, *Surrealism: The Road to the Absolute* (New York: Noonday Press, 1959), pp. 108–09.

5—THE MYTHIC QUEST

1. The stages of the mythical journey are described in Joseph Campbell, *The Hero with a Thousand Faces*, Bollingen Series 27 (Princeton: Princeton University Press, 1972), pp. 49–120.

2. Other signs may be found in "Miranda," from *Sous la lame* (Paris: Gallimard, 1976), pp. 97–112, in which a brutish frontier guard, shortly before his downfall, sees a grasshopper and interprets it as an evil omen; in "Mil neuf cent trente-trois" (*Sous la lame*, pp. 7–76), in which Abel Foligno hears the old woman who admits him to the brothel mutter *alla malora*; in "Armoire de lune," from *Mascarets* (Paris: Gallimard, 1971), pp. 93–108, in which two people who are later swallowed by a tomb fail to notice that it has carved on it "Ci-gisent," with a blank space left for names. ("Ci-gisent" means "Here lie"—a plural form indicating that the tomb is reserved for more than one person.) Dreams also convey omens, as in *Isabella Morra* (Paris: Gallimard, 1973), in which the heroine dreams that she is taken prisoner and dragged away, shortly before her brothers bind and torture her; in "Le Triangle

ambigu" (*Mascarets*, pp. 75–92), in which the heroine is warned in a dream that she will kill the male character. Certain other signs and omens will be discussed in the concluding chapter.

3. Campbell, *Hero*, p. 81.

4. Campbell, *Hero*, p. 119. The description of the heroine's quest for and union with the deity is based on pp. 119–20.

5. J. E. Cirlot, *A Dictionary of Symbols*, translated by Jack Sage (New York: Philosophical Library, 1969), p. 180.

6. Ibid., p. 32.

7. Ibid., p. 49.

8. Other versions of the myth may be found in Campbell, *Hero*, pp. 297–99.

9. Joseph Campbell, *The Masks of God: Occidental Mythology* (Harmondsworth: Penguin, 1976), p. 7.

10. This account is based on Campbell, *The Masks of God: Occidental Mythology*, pp. 7, 21, 22, 79–80, 142, 148, 158, 173–74, 228–30, 301–02.

11. André Pieyre de Mandiargues, preface to Leonora Carrington, *Le Cornet Acoustique*, translated by Henri Parisot (Paris: Flammarion, 1974), p. 10.

12. Mercury was also the patron deity of alchemists, and he can be seen here as the messenger who introduces Bettina to the catalyst that produces a sudden, almost alchemical change in her.

13. For a fuller examination of "Les Pierreuses," see Stirling Haig, "André Pieyre de Mandiargues and 'Les Pierreuses,'" *French Review* 39, no. 2 (November 1965): 275–80.

14. See Cirlot, *A Dictionary of Symbols*, p. 328. This tree is also found in the Garden of Eden myth, and, as a symbol of eternal life through the redemption, in the crucifix. Trees also appear in certain other stories by Mandiargues: on the frozen lake in "L'Archéologue," from *Soleil des loups* (Paris: Laffont, 1951), pp. 7–93, in the cave where Captain Idalium of "L'Opéra des falaises" dies (*Soleil des loups*, pp. 171–208), and in the forests and woods described in *Le Lis de mer* (Paris: Folio, 1972), *La Motocyclette* (Paris: Folio, 1973), and *Marbre* (Paris: Laffont, 1977).

15. Other tales also tell of encounters with the deity. In "Isis du Colisée," from *Le Cadran lunaire* (Paris: Gallimard, 1972), pp. 217–26, the goddess takes the form of a statuette discovered when the author unpacks a crate. On her are a variety of customs stamps in Latin, Greek, and Arabic, indicating that she is known in most Mediterranean lands. In "Une rêverie" (*Le Cadran lunaire*, pp. 165–70), Mandiargues recounts a dream in which he is led by a messenger to an island where he discovers a head burning with an icy fire. This head, he realizes, represents "a kind of elemental birth"—in other words, this is the head of the goddess.

16. This account is based on Joseph Campbell, *The Masks of God: Oriental Mythology* (Harmondsworth: Penguin, 1976), pp. 13, 36, 87, 446; *The Masks of God: Creative Mythology* (Harmondsworth: Penguin, 1976), pp. 20, 23, 73–75, 95–96, 145.

17. André Pieyre de Mandiargues, "Texte inédit: Léonora Carrington," *Combat*, 13 avril 1974, p. 2.

18. André Pieyre de Mandiargues, "Joyce Mansour: Les Gisants satisfaits," *La Nouvelle Nouvelle Revue Française* 13 (février 1959): 330.

6—THE USES OF MYTH

1. Joseph Campbell, *The Masks of God: Primitive Mythology* (Harmondsworth: Penguin, 1976), p. 179.

2. Mircea Eliade, *Images and Symbols. Studies in Religious Symbolism* (New York: Sheed and Ward, 1969), p. 57. Italics in original.

3. Ibid., p. 58.

4. Ibid., p. 57.

5. Joseph Campbell, *The Hero with a Thousand Faces*, Bollingen Series 27 (Princeton: Princeton University Press, 1972), pp. 40–42.

6. See J. E. Cirlot, *A Dictionary of Symbols*, translated by Jack Sage (New York: Philosophical Library, 1962), p. 197.

7. See Campbell, *The Masks of God: Primitive Mythology*, p. 70.

8. Ibid., pp. 64–66.

9. Carl G. Jung, *The Symbolic Life*, translated by R. F. C. Hull, *The Collected Works*, vol. 18 (Princeton: Princeton University Press, 1976), p. 577.

10. Ibid., p. 178.

11. Campbell, *The Masks of God: Primitive Mythology*, p. 315.

12. Campbell, *Hero*, p. 114.

13. Campbell, *The Masks of God: Primitive Mythology*, pp. 104, and 109; *The Masks of God: Occidental Mythology* (Harmondsworth: Penguin, 1976), pp. 13, 112, 309.

14. See Campbell, *The Masks of God: Occidental Mythology*, pp. 518–23; *The Masks of God: Creative Mythology* (Harmondsworth: Penguin, 1976), pp. 4–53, 608–24.

15. See Campbell, *Hero*, p. 21.

16. Carl G. Jung, "Approaching the Unconscious," in *Man and his Symbols*, edited by Carl G. Jung (Garden City: Doubleday, 1976), p. 21.

7—THE JOURNEY INWARDS

1. Quoted in Robert Poulet, "André Pieyre de Mandiargues ou le romantique déniaisé," *Ecrits de Paris*, octobre 1963, p. 94.

2. Alain Jouffroy, "Entretien: Mandiargues, celui qui a fait peur aux jurys," *L'Express*, 6 décembre 1963, p. 43.

3. See *Le Désordre de la mémoire* (Paris: Gallimard, 1975), p. 188, and Jean-Louis de Rambures, "Comment travaillent les écrivains?" *Le Monde [des Livres]*, 25 avril 1970, p. viii.

4. Bettina Knapp, "André Pieyre de Mandiargues," in *French Novelists Speak Out*, edited by Bettina Knapp (Troy, N.Y.: Whitston, 1976), p. 54. Italics in original.

5. Mandiargues's reply to "Notre enquête sur Jean-Jacques Rousseau," *Le Thyrse* 4, no. 2 (1 février 1961): 98.

6. André Pieyre de Mandiargues, "Le poète fait son portrait en écrivant," *Marginales* 125 (avril 1967): 13–14.

7. *Le Désordre de la mémoire*, p. 179. The difference between Mandiargues's technique and automatic writing is that Mandiargues uses a directed reverie, i.e., the intelligence clearly plays some role.

8. Joseph Campbell, *The Masks of God: Occidental Mythology* (Harmondsworth: Penguin, 1976), p. 521.

9. Joseph Campbell, *The Hero with a Thousand Faces*, Bollingen Series 27 (Princeton: Princeton University Press, 1972), p. 29.

10. Campbell, *The Masks of God: Occidental Mythology*, p. 312.

11. André Malraux, *Saturne* (Paris: Gallimard, 1950), p. 110, and "L'Homme et le fantôme," *L'Express*, 21 mai 1955, p. 15.

12. André Pieyre de Mandiargues, "Don C. Talayevsa: *Soleil Hopi*," *La Nouvelle Nouvelle Revue Française* 14 (septembre 1959): 537.

13. André Pieyre de Mandiargues, "Joyce Mansour: *Les Gisants satisfaits*," *La Nouvelle Nouvelle Revue Française* 13 (février 1959): 330.

14. Ibid.

15. It should be noted that the rabbit, which represents Marceline's innocence, is kept well out of the reach of "horrors that the night is said to be capable of producing, and the merest idea of which makes children about to fall asleep break into a sweat: the fox, the marten, the polecat, long supple beasts that slither everywhere in the darkness and which one never sees, which smell strongly and leave bloodless corpses behind them" [*Le Musée noir* (Paris: Folio, 1974), pp. 18–19]. These creatures represent man's instinctual urges, which Marceline encounters once her innocence is destroyed.

16. The girl is another goddess figure: she is reminiscent of an "ancient and fabulous Egypt" [*Sous la lame* (Paris: Gallimard, 1976), p. 102], and she claims that, like the moon, she is a mirror of the sun.

17. André Pieyre de Mandiargues, "C'est le poésie qu'on assassine," *Les Nouvelles Littéraires*, 6–12 mai 1974, p. 21.

18. Other traces of an incestuous theme may be found in "Le Diamant," from *Feu de braise* (Paris: Grasset, 1959), pp. 143–86, where Sarah's father peers into the diamond as Sarah couples with the lion man, filling her view with his image; and in "L'Enfantillage" (*Feu de braise*, pp. 187–213), when the man, as he has intercourse with the prostitute, thinks of the old woman who looked after him as a child, and who was a mother to him.

19. Joseph Campbell, *The Masks of God: Primitive Mythology* (Harmondsworth: Penguin, 1976), pp. 65–66.

20. Frieda Fordham, *An Introduction to Jung's Psychology*, 3rd ed. (Harmondsworth: Penguin, 1976), p. 54.

21. Ibid., p. 62.

22. Ibid., p. 63.

23. Campbell, *Hero*, p. 386. This idea differs from Christianity, which, although it says that "the kingdom of God is within you" (Luke 17: 21), sees the self as so corrupt that it can achieve no contact with God by itself, but only through God's mercy and the redeeming blood of Christ.

24. Carl G. Jung, *Memories, Dreams, Reflections*, translated by Richard and Clara Wilson (New York: Pantheon, 1963), p. 340.

25. Campbell, *Hero*, p. 40.

26. André Pieyre de Mandiargues, "Inédit: Hommage à la rose," *Le Figaro*, 6 novembre 1976, p. 17.

8—REALISM AND FANTASY

1. Quotations taken, respectively, from: Gerda Zeltner, *La Grande Aventure du roman français au XXe siècle* (Paris: Société Nouvelle des Editions Gonthier, 1967), p. 126; Arnold de Kerchove, "René Fallet, Louise de Vilmorin et André Pieyre de Mandiargues," *Revue Générale* 8 (1971): 108; Francine Mallet, Preface to *Le Désordre de la mémoire* (Paris: Gallimard, 1975), p. 38; André Gascht, "André Pieyre de Mandiargues, un réaliste de l'imaginaire," *Biblio* 34, no. 9 (novembre 1966): 3.

2. Quoted by Gascht, "André Pieyre de Mandiargues, un réaliste de l'imaginaire," Biblio 34, no. 9 (novembre 1966): 6.

3. Alain Jouffroy, "Entretien: Mandiargues, celui qui a fait peur aux jurys," *L'Express*, 6 décembre 1963, p. 44.

4. Jean-Louis de Rambures, "Comment travaillent les écrivains?" *Le Monde [des Livres]*, 25 avril 1970, p. viii.

5. André Pieyre de Mandiargues, *Arcimboldo le merveilleux* (Paris: Laffont, 1977), p. 32.

6. Marcel Arland, "Les Contes fantastiques de Pieyre de Mandiargues," in *Nouvelles Lettres de France* (Paris: Albin Michel, 1954), p. 58.

7. Roger Régent, "Goncourt, moto et cinéma," *Les Nouvelles Littéraires*, 21 décembre 1967, p. 14.

8. André Pieyre de Mandiargues, Preface to Marcel Béalu, *L'Araignée d'eau et autres écrits fantastiques* (Paris: Nouvel Office d'Edition, 1964), p. 8.

9. Rambures, "Comment travaillent les écrivains?" p. viii.

10. Bettina Knapp, "André Pieyre de Mandiargues," in *French Novelists Speak Out*, edited by Bettina Knapp (Troy, N.Y.: Whitston, 1976), p. 49.

11. J. H. Matthews, "Zola et les surréalistes," *Les Cahiers Naturalistes*, nos. 24–25 (1963): 99–107.

12. Jouffroy, "Entretien: Mandiargues," *L'Express*, 6 décembre 1963, p. 45.

13. Pierre Mabille, *Le Miroir du merveilleux* (Paris: Les Editions de Minuit, 1962), p. 26.

14. Jouffroy, "Entretien: Mandiargues," *L'Express*, 6 décembre 1963, p. 43.

15. See "Les Chefs-d'œuvre aux terrains vagues," *Le Belvédère* (Paris: Grasset, 1958), pp. 7–19; "Le Corps étranger," and "Les Lis de mer," *Le Cadran lunaire* (Paris: Gallimard, 1972), pp. 15–20 and 26–31.

16. *Le Cadran lunaire*, p. 155. André Breton also talks of this advice from Leonardo in *Point du jour*, Nouvelle édition (Paris: Gallimard, 1970), pp. 220–21.

17. Mandiargues does actually refer to this technique of Magritte's in "La Révolution dans l'image," *Troisième Belvédère* (Paris: Gallimard, 1971), pp. 108–10.

18. Mandiargues does, in fact, compare Dada to shamanism. See *Deuxième Belvédère* (Paris: Grasset, 1962), p. 98.

19. Mircea Eliade, *Images and Symbols. Studies in Religious Symbolism* (New York: Sheed and Ward, 1969), p. 179.

20. André Pieyre de Mandiargues, "Savoir-vivre," *La Nouvelle Revue Française* 37 (juin 1971): 72–75.

21. Sigismond sees the lottery ticket seller again, imagines himself under a shroud, notices a woman whose face reminds him of a death's head, and seems to see shrouds on the flower sellers' kiosks. Rebecca sees a car that reminds her of a coffin, a convoy of soldiers with their instruments of death, a service station resembling a mausoleum, a pump attendant dressed in red, and a child with a crow perched on its hand. In "Miranda," from *Sous la lame* (Paris: Gallimard, 1976), pp. 97–112, a grasshopper is seen as an evil omen. The words "Ci-gisent" on the tomb in *Armoire de lune*, from *Mascarets* (Paris: Gallimard, 1971), pp. 93–108, serve the same purpose. Isabella Morra's dreams also warn of future disasters in *Isabella Morra* (Paris: Gallimard, 1973).

22. André Pieyre de Mandiargues, *Sugaï* (Paris: Georges Fall, 1960), p. 20.

23. Mandiargues's reply to "Notre enquête sur Jean-Jacques Rousseau," *Le Thyrse* 4, no. 21 (1 février 1961): 98.

24. Jouffroy, "Entretien: Mandiargues," *L'Express*, 6 décembre 1963, p. 43.

25. In fact, as Walter Kaufmann points out, Nietzsche tended to use the term "Dionysian" to describe the combination of the two modes in his later work. See Walter Kaufmann, *Nietzsche: Philosopher, Psychologist, Antichrist*, 3rd. ed. (New York: Vintage Books, 1968), pp. 128–30, 152–56.

9—MANDIARGUES'S PLACE IN MODERN LITERATURE

1. Bettina Knapp, "André Pieyre de Mandiargues," in *French Novelists Speak Out*, edited by Bettina Knapp (Troy, N.Y.: Whitston, 1976), p. 53.

2. Jean-Louis de Rambures, "Comment travaillent les écrivains?" *Le Monde [des Livres]*, 25 avril 1970, p. viii.

3. Alain Robbe-Grillet, *Pour un nouveau roman* (Paris: Gallimard, 1963), p. 65.

4. Albert Camus, *Le Mythe de Sisyphe* (Paris: Gallimard, 1942), p. 28.

5. René Lacôte, "Une rencontre avec André Pieyre de Mandiargues," *Les Lettres Françaises*, 6 décembre 1967, p. 3.

6. Louis Aragon, *Entretiens avec François Crémieux* (Paris: Gallimard, 1964), p. 17.

7. J. H. Matthews, *Toward the Poetics of Surrealism* (Syracuse: Syracuse University Press, 1976), p. 12.

8. André Breton, *La Clef des champs* (Paris: Sagittaire, 1953), p. 19.

9. J. H. Matthews, *An Introduction to Surrealism* (University Park: Pennsylvania State University Press, 1965), p. 119.

10. C. W. E. Bigsby, *Dada and Surrealism* (London: Methuen, 1972), p. 66.

11. André Breton, *Point du jour*, nouvelle édition (Paris: Gallimard, 1970), p. 58.

12. André Breton, *L'Amour fou* (Paris: Gallimard, 1937), p. 131.

13. Quoted by Matthews, *An Introduction to Surrealism*, p. 153.

14. The question of the surrealists' political revolt and their sympathies with communism is too complex to go into here. However, their generally leftist beliefs are shared by Mandiargues, who has, as pointed out in Chapter 1, praised the French Communist Party and communist régimes in various parts of the world.

15. Alain Jouffroy, "Entretien: Mandiargues, celui qui a fait peur aux jurys," *L'Express*, 6 décembre 1963, p. 44.

16. André Breton, *Les Manifestes du surréalisme* (Paris: Jean-Jacques Pauvert, 1962), p. 35.

17. A very detailed examination of "Le passage Pommeraye" as a "remake" of *Le Paysan de Paris* may be found in Claude Leroy, "Le Passage Mandiargues," *Cahiers du Vingtième Siècle* 6 (1976): 87–109.

18. Knapp, "André Pieyre de Mandiargues," in *French Novelists*, p. 49.

19. Matthews, *An Introduction to Surrealism*, p. 94.

20. Quoted by Robert Poulet, "André Pieyre de Mandiargues ou le romantique déniaisé," *Ecrits de Paris*, octobre 1963, p. 96.

21. Lacôte, "Une rencontre avec Mandiargues," *Les Lettres Françaises*, 6 décembre 1967, p. 4.

22. André Pieyre de Mandiargues, "*Un Rêve plus long que la nuit*, par Alain Jouffroy," *L'Express*, 7 november 1963, p. 44.

23. André Breton, *Entretiens (1913–1952)* (Paris: Gallimard, 1969), p. 281.

24. Carl G. Jung, *The Structure and Dynamics of the Psyche*, translated by R. F. C. Hull, 2nd. ed., *The Collected Works*, vol. 8 (Princeton: Princeton University Press, 1969), p. 310.

25. Mircea Eliade, *Images and Symbols. Studies in Religious Symbolism* (New York: Sheed and Ward, 1969), p. 13.

26. Frieda Fordham, *An Introduction to Jung's Psychology*, 3rd. ed. (Harmondsworth: Penguin, 1976), p. 27. This paragraph is based on Joseph Campbell, *The Masks of God: Primitive Mythology* (Harmondsworth: Penguin, 1976), pp. 57–88.

27. Campbell, *The Masks of God: Primitive Mythology*, p. 42.

28. Jouffroy, "Entretien: Mandiargues," *L'Express*, 6 décembre 1963, p. 43.

29. See J. H. Matthews, *Surrealism and the Novel* (Ann Arbor: University of Michigan Press, 1966), p. 93.

30. Campbell, *The Masks of God: Primitive Mythology*, p. 253.

Bibliography

WORKS BY ANDRÉ PIEYRE DE MANDIARGUES

Major Works

The following list shows the original date of publication and original publisher. When I have used a different edition for this study, it is indicated after the first entry for that title. I have not included here numerous prefaces, translations, and exhibition catalogues by Mandiargues.

Dans les années sordides. Monaco: A.P.M., 1943.

Hedera, ou la persistance de l'amour pendant une rêverie. Monaco: Hommage, 1945.

Les Incongruités monumentales. Paris: Laffont, 1946.

L'Etudiante. Paris: Fontaine, 1946.

Le Musée noir. Paris: Laffont, 1946. (Edition used here published by Gallimard in the "Folio" collection in 1974).

Les Sept périls spectraux. Lithographies de Dorothea Tanning. Paris: Les Pas Perdus, 1950.

Soleil des loups. Paris: Laffont, 1951.

Marbre. Paris: Laffont, 1953. (Edition used here published in 1977 by Laffont).

Astyanax. Desseins de Bona. Paris: Le Terrain Vague, 1956.

Le Lis de mer. Paris: Laffont, 1956. (Edition used here published by Gallimard in the "Folio" collection in 1972).

Les Monstres de Bomarzo. Photographies de Glasberg. Paris: Grasset, 1957.

Le Belvédère. Paris: Grasset, 1958.

Le Cadran lunaire. Paris: Laffont, 1958. (Edition used here published by Gallimard in 1972).

Feu de braise. Paris: Grasset, 1959.

Cartolines et dédicaces. Paris: Le Terrain Vague, 1960.

Sugaï. Paris: Georges Fall, 1960.

L'Age de craie, suivi de Hedera. Paris: Gallimard, 1961.

Deuxième Belvédère. Paris: Grasset, 1962.

La Nuit l'amour. Eaux-fortes de Bernard Dufour. Paris: Pierre Loeb, 1962.

La Motocyclette. Paris: Gallimard, 1963. (Edition used here published by Gallimard in the "Folio" collection in 1973).

Le Point où j'en suis, suivi de Dalila exaltée et de la Nuit l'amour. Paris: Gallimard, 1964.

Astyanax, précédé de Les Incongruités monumentales et suivi de Cartolines et dédicaces. Paris: Gallimard, 1964.

Beylamour. Paris: J.-J. Pauvert, 1965.

Les Corps illuminés. Photographies de Frédéric Barzilay. Paris: Mercure de France, 1965.

Larmes de généraux. Lithographies de Baj. Stockholm: Herman Igell, 1965.

Porte dévergondée. Paris: Gallimard, 1965.

L'Age de craie, suivi de Dans les années sordides et de Hedera. Paris: Gallimard, 1967.

Critiquettes. Eaux-fortes de Bona. Montpellier: Fata Morgana, 1967.

Jacinthes. Eaux-fortes d'Alexandre Bonnier. Paris: O. Lazar-Vernet, 1967.

La Marge. Paris: Gallimard, 1967.

Le Marronnier. Paris: Mercure de France, 1968.

Ruisseau des solitudes, suivi de Jacinthes et de Chapeaugaga. Paris: Gallimard, 1968.

Le Lièvre de la lune. Eaux-fortes de Baj. Milan: M'Arte, 1970.

Eros solaire. Desseins érotiques, lithographies d'André Masson. Paris: Tchou, 1970.

Bona l'amour et la peinture. Geneva: Skira, 1971.

La Nuit de mil neuf cent quatorze, ou le style liberty. Paris: L'Herne, 1970.

Troisième Belvédère. Paris: Gallimard, 1971.

Mascarets. Paris: Gallimard, 1971.

Croiseur noir. Eaux-fortes de Lam. Paris: O. Lazar-Vernet, 1972.

Isabella Morra. Paris: Gallimard, 1973.

Terre érotique. Lithographies d'André Masson. Paris: Tchou, 1974.

Chagall. Paris: Maeght, 1975.

Le Désordre de la mémoire. Entretiens avec Francine Mallet. Paris: Gallimard, 1975.

Sous la lame. Paris: Gallimard, 1976.

Parapapillonneries. Lithographies de Meret Oppenheim. Paris: Casset, 1976.

Arcimboldo le merveilleux. Paris: Laffont, 1977.

L'Anglais décrit dans le château fermé. Paris: Gallimard, 1979. (Previously published under the pseudonym Pierre Morion by Oxford and Cambridge in 1953 and by L'Or du Temps in 1969.)

L'Ivre œil, suivi de Croiseur noir et de Passage de l'Egyptienne. Paris: Gallimard, 1979.

La Nuit séculaire. Paris: Gallimard, 1979.

Works by Mandiargues Translated into English

The Girl Beneath the Lion (Le Lis de mer). Translated by Richard Howard. New York: Grove Press, 1958.

The Motorcycle. Translated by Richard Howard. New York: Grove Press, 1965.

The Girl on the Motorcycle. Translated by Alexander Trocchi. London: Calder and Boyars, 1966.

Hyacinths (Jacinthes). Translated by Edward Lucie Smith. Paris: Olv, 1967.

The Margin. Translated by Richard Howard. New York: Grove Press, 1969.

Blaze of Embers (Feu de braise). Translated by April Fitzlyon. London: Calder and Boyars, 1971.
Arcimboldo the Marvelous. Translated by Mark Paris. New York: Abrahams, 1978.

Articles and Prefaces by André Pieyre de Mandiargues Quoted in This Study

Preface to *Les Masques de Léonor Fini*. Photographies d'André Ostier. Paris: La Parade, 1951.
"Hans Bellmer: *Anatomie de l'image*." *La Nouvelle Nouvelle Revue Française* 10, no. 59 (novembre 1957): 973–74.
"Joyce Mansour: *Les Gisants satisfaits*." *La Nouvelle Nouvelle Revue Française* 13, no. 74 (février 1959): 330–31.
"Don C. Talayesva: *Soleil Hopi*." *La Nouvelle Nouvelle Revue Française* 14, no. 18 (septembre 1959): 535–37.
"Alfonso Reyes." *La Nouvelle Nouvelle Revue Française* 15, no. 86 (février 1960): 346–47.
Mandiargues's reply to "Notre enquête sur Jean-Jacques Rousseau." *Le Thyrse* 4, no. 2 (1 février 1961): 98.
"D'Aurélia à Mona." *L'Express*, 7 novembre 1963, p. 44.
Preface to *L'Araignée d'eau et autres écrits fantastiques* by Marcel Béalu. Paris: Nouvel Office d'Edition, 1964.
"Le Poète fait son portrait en écrivant." *Marginales* 125 (avril 1967): 13–14.
"Savoir-vivre." *La Nouvelle Revue Française* 37, no. 222 (juin 1971): 72–75.
Preface to *Le Cornet acoustique* by Leonora Carrington. Translated by Henri Parisot. Paris: Flammarion, 1974.
"Texte inédit: Leonora Carrington." *Combat*, 13 avril 1974, p. 2.
"C'est la poésie qu'on assassine." *Les Nouvelles Littéraires*, 6–12 mai 1974, p. 21.
"Inédit: Hommage à la rose." *Le Figaro*, 6 novembre 1976, p. 17.

CRITICAL WORKS ON ANDRÉ PIEYRE DE MANDIARGUES

The following list includes all critical material mentioned in the course of this study. Certain other items which may be consulted with profit are included. There are numerous book reviews and some articles which I have not listed.

Abirached, Robert. "D'un merveilleux moderne." *La Nouvelle Revue Française* 21, no. 126 (juin 1963): 1070–75.
Alyn, Marc. "André Pieyre de Mandiargues: *L'Age de craie*." *La Table Ronde*, no. 172 (mai 1962): 119–20.
Arland, Marcel. "Les Contes fantastiques de Pieyre de Mandiargues." In *Nouvelles Lettres de France*, pp. 53–63. Paris: Albin Michel, 1954.
Bond, David J. "André Pieyre de Mandiargues and the Discovery of the Self." *The International Fiction Review* 6, no. 2 (Summer 1979): 133–36.

————. "André Pieyre de Mandiargues: Some Ideas on Art." *Romanic Review* 70, no. 1 (January 1979): 69–79.

————. "Mystic and Erotic Experience in the Fiction of André Pieyre de Mandiargues." *Kentucky Romance Quarterly* 27, no. 2 (1980): 205–13.

————. "Recurring Patterns of Fantasy in the Fiction of André Pieyre de Mandiargues." *Symposium* 29, nos. 1–2 (Spring–Summer 1975): 30–47.

Bonnefoy, Claude. "Pieyre de Mandiargues." In *Dictionnaire de la littérature française contemporaine*, edited by Claude Bonnefoy, Tony Cartano, and Daniel Oster. Paris: Jean-Pierre Delarge, 1977.

Brooks, Peter. "The Pleasure Principle." *Partisan Review* 33, no. 1 (Winter 1966): 128–32.

Cahiers Renaud-Barrault, no. 86 (1974). Contains articles by Julien Gracq, Salah Stétié, and Ornella Volta.

Campanini, Susan. "Alchemy in Pieyre de Mandiargues' 'Le Diamant.'" *French Review* 50, no. 4 (March 1977): 602–09.

Charney, Hanna. "The Tide as Structure in 'La Marée.'" *Dada/Surrealism* 5 (1976): 5–10.

Clerval, Alain. "André Pieyre de Mandiargues: un érotique baroque." *La Nouvelle Revue Française* 38, no. 224 (août 1971): 77–81.

Dedet, Christian. "André Pieyre de Mandiargues, *La Motocyclette*." *La Table Ronde*, no. 193 (février 1964): 142–43.

Elsen, Claude. "Couleurs du fantastique." *La Table Ronde*, no. 44 (août 1951): 146–49.

Gamarra, Pierre. "Les Livres nouveaux." *Europe*, nos. 465–66 (janvier–février 1968): 240–41.

Gascht, André. "André Pieyre de Mandiargues ou le goût de l'insolite." *Marginales*, no. 74 (octobre 1960): 18–33.

————. "André Pieyre de Mandiargues, un réaliste de l'imaginaire." *Biblio* 34, no. 9 (novembre 1966): 3–8.

Habel, Angela. "Eclairer et confondre: Deux fonctions du miroir chez André Pieyre de Mandiargues." *Australian Journal of French Studies* 14, no. 3 (May–August 1977): 189–97.

Haig, Stirling. "André Pieyre de Mandiargues and 'Les Pierreuses.'" *French Review* 39, no. 2 (November 1965): 275–80.

Jouffroy, Alain. "Entretien: Mandiargues, celui qui a fait peur aux jurys." *L'Express*, 6 décembre 1963, pp. 43–44.

Kanters, Robert. "André Pieyre de Mandiargues et la mort en suspens." *Le Figaro Littéraire*, 5–11 juin 1967, pp. 19–20.

————. "André Pieyre de Mandiargues." *La Revue de Paris* 75, no. 1 (janvier 1968): 116–23.

Kayser, Lucien. "Une Poétique plutonienne." *Les Pages de la Société des Ecrivains Luxembourgeois de Langue Française* 17 (1971): 39–54.

Kerchove, Arnold de. "René Fallet, Louise de Vilmorin et André Pieyre de Mandiargues." *Revue Générale* 8 (1971): 103–10.

Knapp, Bettina. "André Pieyre de Mandiargues." In *French Novelists Speak Out*, edited by Bettina Knapp. Troy, N.Y.: Whitston, 1976, pp. 48–56.

Korger, Matthias-E. "Pieyre de Mandiargues et la métamorphose du roman-tisme." *Marginales*, no. 121 (juillet 1968): 1–9.

Lacôte, René. "Une rencontre avec André Pieyre de Mandiargues." *Les Lettres Françaises*, 6–12, décembre 1967, pp. 3–4.

Leroy, Claude. "Le Passage Mandiargues." *Cahiers du Vingtième Siècle* 4 (1976): 87–109.

———. "Mandiargues ou la parade du montreur de textes." *Revue des Sciences Humaines*, no. 167 (1977): 365–77.

Mallet, Francine. "Des *Années sordides* à *La Marge*, l'œuvre de Pieyre de Mandiargues enrichit les mêmes thèmes." *Le Monde [des Livres]*, 3 mai 1967, pp. i–ii.

Nimier, Roger. "André Pieyre de Mandiargues." In *Journées de lectures*. Paris: Gallimard, 1965, pp. 227–29.

d'Ormesson, Jean. "André Pieyre de Mandiargues entre l'art et l'amour." *Les Nouvelles Littéraires*, 14 mai 1971, p. 6.

Paz, Octavio. "The Metamorphoses of Stone." In *Alternating Current*. Translated by Helen R. Lane. New York: Viking, 1973, pp. 91–95.

Poulet, Robert. "André Pieyre de Mandiargues ou le romantique déniaisé." *Ecrits de Paris*, octobre 1963, pp. 91–97.

———. "Suite et fin des faits nouveaux." *Ecrits de Paris*, avril 1969, 91–98.

Rambures, Jean-Louis de. "Comment travaillent les écrivains?" *Le Monde [des Livres]*, 25 avril 1970, p. viii.

Régent, Roger. "Goncourt, moto et cinéma." *Les Nouvelles Littéraires*, 21 décembre 1967, p. 14.

Robin, André. "André Pieyre de Mandiargues ou l'initiation panique. I: La Perversité cosmique." *Cahiers du Sud* 60, nos. 383–84 (août–septembre–octobre 1965): 138–50.

———. "André Pieyre de Mandiargues ou l'initiation panique. II: L'Initiation panique." *Cahiers du Sud* 60, no. 385 (novembre–décembre 1965): 195–313.

Rode, Henri. "Les Romans et les jours." *Marginales* 52 (février 1957): 51–54.

Stétié, Salah. *André Pieyre de Mandiargues*. Paris: Seghers, 1978.

T., C. "Dropping out in all directions." *Observer*, 1 February 1970, p. 30.

Temmer, Mark J. "André Pieyre de Mandiargues." *Yale French Studies* 31 (1964): 99–104.

Teyssèdre, Bernard. "Pieyre de Mandiargues critique d'art?" *Les Lettres Nouvelles*, no. 39 (octobre 1963): 211–21.

Zeltner, Gerda. *La Grande Aventure du roman français au XXᵉ siècle*. Paris: Société Nouvelle des Editions Gonthier, 1967.

GENERAL

The following works were consulted in connection with the general background to this study.

Aragon, Louis. *Entretiens avec François Crémieux*. Paris: Gallimard, 1964.

Balakian, Anna. *Surrealism: The Road to the Absolute*. New York: The Noonday Press, 1959.

Bataille, Georges. *L'Erotisme*. Paris: Les Editions de Minuit, 1957.

Bigsby, C. W. E. *Dada and Surrealism*. London: Methuen, 1972.

Breton, André. *La Clef des champs*. Paris: Sagittaire, 1953.

———. *Entretiens (1913–1952)*. Paris: Gallimard, 1969.

———. *Nadja*. Paris: Gallimard, 1928.

———. *Manifestes du surréalisme*. Paris: J.-J. Pauvert, 1962.

———. *Point du jour*. Nouvelle Edition. Paris: Gallimard, 1970.

Campbell, Joseph. *The Hero with a Thousand Faces*. Bollingen Series 27. Princeton: Princeton University Press, 1972.

———. *The Masks of God: Primitive Mythology*. Harmondsworth: Penguin Books, 1976.

———. *The Masks of God: Oriental Mythology*. Harmondsworth: Penguin Books, 1976.

———. *The Masks of God: Occidental Mythology*. Harmondsworth: Penguin Books, 1976.

———. *The Masks of God: Creative Mythology*. Harmondsworth: Penguin Books, 1976.

Camus, Albert. *Le Mythe de Sisyphe*. Paris: Gallimard, 1942.

Cirlot, J. E. *A Dictionary of Symbols*. Translated by Jack Sage. New York: Philosophical Library, 1962.

Eliade, Mircea. *Images and Symbols. Studies in Religious Symbolism*. New York: Sheed and Ward, 1969.

Fordham, Frieda. *An Introduction to Jung's Psychology*. 3rd ed. Harmondsworth: Penguin Books, 1976.

Jung, Carl G. *Memories, Dreams, Reflections*. Translated by Richard and Clara Wilson. New York: Pantheon Books, 1963.

———. *The Structure and Dynamics of the Psyche*. 2nd ed. Translated by R. F. C. Hull. The Collected Works, vol. 8. Bollingen Series 20. Princeton: Princeton University Press, 1969.

———. *Archetypes and the Collective Unconscious*. 2nd ed. Translated by R. F. C. Hull. The Collected Works, vol. 9. Bollingen Series 20. Princeton: Princeton University Press, 1969.

———. *The Symbolic Life*. Translated by R. F. C. Hull. The Collected Works, vol. 18. Bollingen Series 20. Princeton: Princeton University Press, 1976.

———. "Approaching the Unconscious." In *Man and his Symbols*, edited by Carl G. Jung. Garden City: Doubleday, 1976, pp. 19–103.

Kaufmann, Walter. *Nietzsche: Philosopher, Psychologist, Antichrist*. 3rd ed. New York: Vintage Books, 1968.

Mabille, Pierre. *Le Miroir du merveilleux*. Paris: Les Editions de Minuit, 1962.

Malraux, André. "L'Homme et le fantôme." *L'Express*, 21 mai 1955, p. 15.

———. *Saturne*. Paris: Gallimard, 1950.

Mann, Thomas, "Freud and the Future." In *Essays of Three Decades*. Translated by H. T. Lowe-Porter. New York: Knopf, 1947, pp. 411–28.

Matthews, J. H. *An Introduction to Surrealism*. University Park: Pennsylvania State University Press, 1965.

———. *Surrealism and the Novel*. Ann Arbor: University of Michigan Press, 1966.

———. *Toward the Poetics of Surrealism*. Syracuse: Syracuse University Press, 1976.

———. "Zola et les surréalistes." *Les Cahiers Naturalistes* 24–25 (1963): 99–107.

Robbe-Grillet, Alain. *Pour un nouveau roman*. Paris: Gallimard. 1963.

Schneider, Marcel. *La Littérature fantastique en France*. Paris: Fayard, 1964.

Index

Unconscious, the. *See* Self, depths of
Underworld. *See* Hell
Unusual, the, in Mandiargues's work, xii, 8

Vedantic thought, 59
Venus, 44, 45, 55, 57, 81
Verne, Jules, 2
Vesper, 44, 45
Vian, Boris, 97
Victim, sacrificial. *See* Ritual and sacrifice
Virginity, loss of, 5, 16, 19, 52, 111 n.8
Virgin Mary, 53, 54, 55
Voltaire, 11
Voyant, artist as, xvi, 89–90, 94, 102–104

Walpole, Horace, 98
Wilderness: in myth, 52, 57; as dark reaches of self, 76–77

Williams, William Carlos, 3
Windows as openings on self, 74–75, 81
Witches, 60
Woman: archetype of, in Mandiargues's work, 2; defended by Mandiargues, 111 n.2; as inspiration of Mandiargues's work, 3. *See also* Eroticism, woman in; Marvelous, the, woman as source of
Wotan, 56

Yeats, W. B., 56

Zeus, 37
Zola, Emile, *Au Bonheur des dames; Bête humaine, La; Germinal,* 87
Zurburan, Francisco de, 95
Zürn, Unica, 91

THE FICTION OF ANDRÉ PIEYRE de MANDIARGUES

was composed in 10-point Linotron 202 Caledonia and leaded two points
by Coghill Book Typesetting Co.;
with display type in Deepdene by J. M. Bundscho, Inc.;
printed on 55-pound acid-free Glatfelter Antique Cream,
Smythe-sewn and bound over boards in Joanna Arrestox B,
also adhesive bound with paper covers drawn on
by Maple-Vail Book Manufacturing Group, Inc.,
and published by

SYRACUSE UNIVERSITY PRESS
SYRACUSE, NEW YORK 13210